'FUNDAMENTALISM' AND THE WORD OF GOD

‘FUNDAMENTALISM’ AND THE WORD OF GOD

Some Evangelical Principles

by

J. I. PACKER, M.A., D.Phil.

WM. B. EERDMANS PUBLISHING CO.
GRAND RAPIDS 3, MICHIGAN

First Edition, March 1958
Reprinted, September 1958
Reprinted, December 1958
Reprinted, January 1960
Reprinted, February 1962
Reprinted, May 1964
Reprinted, February 1966
Reprinted, December 1967
Reprinted, August 1970
Reprinted, May 1972

ISBN 0-8028-1147-7

PHOTOLITHOPRINTED BY GRAND RAPIDS BOOK MANUFACTURERS, INC.
GRAND RAPIDS, MICHIGAN

1972

CONTENTS

'Defend the Bible? I would as soon defend a lion.'

C. H. SPURGEON

FOREWORD

THIS book is offered as a constructive re-statement of evangelical principles in the light of the current 'Fundamentalism controversy'. Its aim is to fix the right approach to the Bible, to the intellectual tasks of faith, and to the present debate. If it does that, and if it helps evangelical Christians to understand their faith better and witness to it more effectively, I shall be thankful.

I owe a debt of gratitude to the Rev. R. T. Beckwith, the Rev. J. W. Wenham and Mr. O. R. Johnston for reading these chapters and making many suggestions for their improvement. Most of all, I must thank my wife for her patience and help.

J. I. PACKER

CHAPTER I

'FUNDAMENTALISTS' UNDER FIRE

And it came to pass, when Ahab saw Elijah, that Ahab said unto him, Is it thou, thou troubler of Israel?

1 KINGS xviii. 17, RV

'FUNDAMENTALISM' has recently grown notorious. Three factors seem to have caused this: Billy Graham's evangelistic crusades, the growth of evangelical groups in schools and universities, and the increase of evangelical candidates for the ministry. A long correspondence in *The Times* in August 1955, coupled with strong words from bishops, headmasters and other responsible persons, made 'Fundamentalism' a matter of general interest. Since then, 'anti-fundamentalism' has become a widespread fashion. The debate continues, and shows no sign of abating yet.

It must encourage evangelical Christians to find so much notice taken of their position. The fact that those who differ from them can no longer ignore them marks a real increase in their influence. Unhappily, however, this discussion of their views goes on under what F. L. Patton once described as 'a condition of low visibility'. Crucial terms are used equivocally; questions are not clearly formulated; disputants snipe at each other more or less haphazardly. This is an unhelpful state of affairs, for low visibility leads to argument at cross purposes, and cross purposes stultify argument altogether. The following pages have been written in an attempt to resolve some of the misunderstandings that have arisen and with the aim of showing what is really at stake in this controversy.

VARIED CRITICISMS

Consider first how its critics picture 'Fundamentalism'. They have two main ways of doing this, neither of which is adequate.

Sometimes they define it as a theological peculiarity; namely, adherence to a distinctive doctrine of Scripture. But they are not then unanimous as to what that doctrine is. Professor Alan Richardson, for instance, in the 1950 edition of *Chambers' Encyclopædia* described 'Fundamentalism' as a view about the *origin* of the Bible—'the theory of biblical inspiration which regards the written words of the Bible as divinely dictated'.[1] The Bishop of Rochester, however, in a sermon printed in *Theology* for March 1956 (since published separately), defined 'Fundamentalism' as a view about the *nature* of the Bible—'the verbal inerrancy of Holy Scripture'; while the author of the leading article which ended *The Times* correspondence pictured it as a view about the *interpretation* of the Bible, describing a 'Fundamentalist' as 'a theologian who holds that every word of them (the Scriptures) should be treated as factually true'. Some elaborate this last point by adding that these 'Fundamentalists' have an authoritarian cast of mind and compel their disciples to subscribe to all the peculiarities of their exegesis. Thus, Gabriel Hebert makes the extraordinary statement: 'The "Jehovah's Witnesses" and the "Seventh Day Adventists" are Fundamentalists *in the strict sense*[2] since they assume the complete infallibility and inerrancy of the text of the Bible, and add interpretations of their own which are imposed as of obligation on their adherents.'[3] Such a remark is, in fact, a complete *reductio ad absurdum* of the idea that the distinguishing mark of evangelical Christianity (which is what all these writers are trying to talk about) is its adherence to any or all of the opinions listed above. A criterion which fails to differentiate evangelical Christians from non-Christian groups like Jehovah's Witnesses is plainly inadequate. Some other definition is required.

Sometimes a broader picture is painted. 'Fundamentalism' is then depicted as a religious phenomenon, distinguished not merely by its queer doctrine of Scripture, but also by certain peculiarities of practice. Dr. Michael

[1] For an extended note on this article, see Appendix I, pp. 178 ff.
[2] Italics ours. Who, we wonder, fixed this 'strict sense'?
[3] *Fundamentalism and the Church of God* (S.C.M., 1957), p. 22.

Ramsey, for instance, writing in *The Bishoprick* (the Durham diocesan magazine) in February 1956, described 'Fundamentalism' as 'a version of Christianity with certain closely knit features' which he listed as follows: a denial of the human element in the Bible; a belief in the penal doctrine of the atonement; a habit of appealing for immediate decision at the close of evangelistic sermons; and an individualistic doctrine of the Holy Spirit's work in the believer which makes churchmanship and sacraments practically superfluous. Gabriel Hebert, in the book already cited, suggests that the evangelical movement is disfigured chiefly by two things: an inadequate doctrine of the Bible, and a proud attitude of spiritual self-sufficiency.[1] Others give other lists of its failings. Liberals blame 'Fundamentalists' for not being Liberals; sacramentalists for not being sacramentalists; neo-orthodox for not being neo-orthodox; and so on. The limitation of this kind of criticism is clear. It tells us, in terms of some other system, what 'Fundamentalism' is not, without telling us—often, indeed, without even asking—what 'Fundamentalism' is in terms of itself. Consequently, these accounts do not touch the heart of the matter; for 'Fundamentalism' is something quite different from these other systems, and can be understood only in terms of its own first principles.

There is one point, however, on which all 'anti-fundamentalists' seem to agree; that is, that the doctrine of Scripture which they attribute to their evangelical brethren (whether they define it as dictation, literalism, inerrancy or anything else) is new, eccentric and in reality untenable. They note that the word 'Fundamentalism' is a twentieth-century coinage, and conclude that the thing is as new as its name. It began, they say, as a reaction against literary and historical criticism of the Bible, and attacks launched in the name of science against what the Bible was thought to teach about creation. It represents a defiant hardening of pre-critical and pre-scientific views, a desperate attempt to bolster up obsolete traditions. As such, it is a flight from facts. It provides a bolt-hole from

[1] *Op. cit.*; see Chapters IV–VII, VIII, IX.

the present to the past. In order to be a 'Fundamentalist', one must keep one's mind resolutely closed—locked, bolted and barred—against the entry of modern knowledge about the Bible. 'Fundamentalism' is thus retrograde and, in effect, dishonest. 'Intellectual hara-kiri' (to quote a correspondent to *The Times*) is the price which it exacts of its adherents; they have to learn to turn a blind eye to plain facts. This is why 'Fundamentalism' is so often equated with obscurantism, which the *Shorter Oxford Dictionary* defines as 'the practice or principles of those who strive to prevent enlightenment or the progress of knowledge'. The critics of 'Fundamentalism' see it as one among the many movements of blind reaction which disfigure the record of man's intellectual history; it presents to them the all-too-familiar spectacle of a die-hard traditionalism refusing to confess itself out-of-date. And in the heat of its reaction, they think, it has lost all balance of judgment. Some truths it runs to death, others it neglects entirely, and those who cannot say all its shibboleths it damns out of hand. 'It is *heretical*,' Dr. Ramsey declares, 'in one of the classic meanings of heresy, in that it represents a fixation of distorted elements from the Bible without the balanced tradition of scriptural truth as a whole. It is *sectarian*, in that the ardent Fundamentalist has no regard for religion outside his own experience and vocabulary.' As its critics see it, therefore 'Fundamentalism' holds out no promise for the future; it can do only harm while it lives; and the best that can be hoped for is that it may die decently and soon.

Naturally, those who take this view of the matter are deeply and sincerely distressed to see how vigorously 'Fundamentalists' labour to win young people to their faith. Such work, they fear, must in the long run do more harm than good. Their anxiety on this point was forthrightly voiced in the letter deploring Billy Graham's Cambridge mission with which the correspondence in *The Times* began. 'Universities exist for the advancement of learning,' said the letter; 'on what basis, therefore, can fundamentalism claim a hearing at Cambridge? In other spheres . . . an approach which pays no heed to the work of modern scholarship is unthinkable before a university audience. . . . Is it not time that our religious leaders made it plain that . . . they cannot regard fundamentalism as likely to issue in anything but disillusionment and disaster for educated men and women in this twentieth-century world?"[1] A movement that is essentially obscurantist must inevitably be hostile to the best interests of Christian scholarship and education; and this, it is said, means that 'Fundamentalism' is a menace to the very work of evangelism which it so energetically sponsors. The robust and unhesitating acceptance by the 'fundamentalist' preacher of what 'the Bible says' imparts to his message an attractive note of certainty and authority. This is just what alarms those who criticize this approach to evangelism; for biblical authority as 'Fundamentalists' understand it cannot, they think, be honestly maintained. To demand unquestioning submission to what 'the Bible says' seems to them tantamount to telling men to crucify their reason; such an attitude to the Bible, they think, is superstitious rather than religious, and bibliolatrous rather than Christian.

That 'Fundamentalists' do in fact tell men to crucify their reason is very obvious, such critics say, from their technique of evangelism. They meet intellectual difficulties, not with argument, but with authority; the claims of reason are brushed aside and enquirers are directed, on the sole basis of what 'the Bible says', to an act of blind 'decision', in which (they are told) the answer to all their problems will somehow magically be found. It is precisely in this crude but cavalier dogmatism, it is supposed, that the appeal of the 'fundamentalist' gospel lies. It cannot be denied that this gospel works a remarkable transformation in the lives of very many; but this is attributed not to the force of truth, but to the attraction of an authoritarian system. For adolescents this attraction is particularly strong, and particularly harmful. Dr. Ramsey expresses himself on this subject with vigour. '"Fundamentalist" evangelism', he writes, 'produces an ardent discipleship often marked by zeal and self-sacrifice. And why? It

[1] *The Times*, August 15, 1955.

offers authority and security, quick and sure, to a generation restless and insecure. Other and more wholesome versions of Christianity offer security indeed—but rather more slowly. . . . But here is security—in a single night. Hither, young man, drown your worries in the rapture of conversion: stifle your doubts by abdicating the use of your mind. A rousing sermon, a hurricane of emotion, a will to leap in the dark—and peace at once and for ever.' That, at any rate, is what this escapist gospel promises; but 'the stifling of the mind in the process of decision may bring the most terrible revenges in scepticism and disillusion'.[1] And this, Dr. Ramsey thinks, is often the result of the evangelism of 'Fundamentalists'; for it seems to him an essential part of their gospel that man must renounce the guidance of reason in order to embrace an unreasonable bibliolatry.

THE NEED FOR AN ANSWER

Thus the critics generally interpret and evaluate what Dr. Ramsey calls 'our English fundamentalism'. Naturally, they are not too respectful towards it. There is no doubt whom they have in mind in all this; it is the evangelical movement as a whole that is under fire. Hebert, in his book, is quite explicit: 'conservative evangelicals in the Church of England and other churches, and . . . the Inter-Varsity Fellowship of Evangelical Unions' are the persons to whom, and of whom, he is speaking.[2] Now what should the reaction of Evangelicals be? Their critics' interpretation of Evangelicalism is, in their opinion, demonstrably false, and the strictures based on it are invalid. But theological controversy is an arid business, and 'anti-fundamentalism' is a fashion that may soon pass, as so many other fashions in theology have done. Might it not be wiser to ignore the whole thing?

There are at least two reasons why it would be wrong to pass over these criticisms in silence.

In the first place, they are made in good faith. They spring from a serious concern for Christian education and scholarship, for pastoral and evangelistic work in schools

[1] *Op. cit.*, p. 25. [2] *Op. cit.*, p. 10.

and colleges, for the welfare of the world Church. Such concern is right, and Evangelicals respect it; indeed, they share it. If, therefore, they think that their critics' fears are groundless, it is their duty to allay them. Furthermore, if they think that it is the principles of their critics, rather than those of Evangelicalism, which endanger the interests that we all have at heart, then they ought to say so. But they do think these things. That is one reason why this book is being written.

In the second place, these criticisms go deep. If they were concerned only with current evangelical practice, they would not much matter. Indeed, they would be rather comic; for it is not hard to show that the descriptions of evangelical practice which are being put forward are somewhat wide of the mark. Dr. Ramsey's picture of 'fundamentalist' evangelism, for instance, to which we referred above, is a caricature, as J. R. W. Stott showed in his booklet, *Fundamentalism and Evangelism.*[1] But, in fact, these criticisms are directed rather at evangelical principles than at evangelical practice. We dismiss them too lightly if we do not see this. Why is Dr. Ramsey's description of 'fundamentalist' evangelism such a caricature? Simply because it is partly an interpretation of the practice in terms of what he regards as the principle underlying it. He considers the uncompromising demand for submission to what 'the Bible says', because the Bible says it, to be essentially unreasonable. Therefore, he interprets the appeal for 'decision' on this basis as being, in effect, a command to stifle the mind. His judgment of the practice is determined by his view of the principle. So it is with the other critics generally. Their real case is that 'Fundamentalism' is founded on a false principle—the exploded notion of biblical inerrancy. This is to say, in effect, that Evangelicalism is a form of Christianity that cannot honestly be held today. Such an indictment surely calls for comment by those who believe the evangelical faith to be the revealed truth of God. This is a further reason why it seemed needful to write this book.

[1] Published by *Crusade*, 30 Bedford Place, W.C.1.

A FALSE ANALYSIS

What, then, are the real questions at issue? and how should we set about discussing them?

Here we are confronted with a remarkable fact. When 'anti-fundamentalists' generalize about 'Fundamentalism', they use, as we saw, very strong language; they describe it as 'obscurantist', 'heretical', 'sectarian', 'schismatic', 'crude' and 'atavistic', and its influence as 'disastrous'. Nothing seems too bad to say about it! But when, after this, they come down to details, they are suddenly found assuring us that there is no substantial difference between Evangelicals and themselves at all! This strange *volte-face* is worth looking into.

The critics (at least, the more charitable and balanced of them) normally argue somewhat as follows: 'The first thing to grasp,' they say, 'is that these "Fundamentalists" are essentially orthodox in their beliefs and admirably forthright in their witness to basic Christian truth.[1] But, unfortunately, there seem to be gaps in the evangelical understanding of the gospel (on such matters as the Church, the sacraments, and the meaning of Christian witness in society); and there are crudities too (such as this obscurantist attitude to the Bible, which casts a black shadow over all evangelical theology). Because of these ugly disfigurements, it is proper to call "Fundamentalism" heretical. But "Fundamentalists" do not err on anything essential, and a few minor adjustments of certain points in their teaching would put them right.' From this analysis they go on to draw the following conclusion. 'It appears,' they say, 'that there is no valid reason why evangelical groups should stand apart from such bodies

[1] 'Both sides hold the orthodox faith,' says Hebert (*op cit.*, p. 12); and Philip Lee-Woolf, a former General Secretary of the Student Christian Movement, writes thus: 'I do not think that the centre of the controversy is doctrinal in the ordinary sense. As a whole, and at their best, conservative Evangelicals lay splendid stress upon the fundamentals of the Christian revelation . . . the great pivots are there—sin and grace, revelation and Jesus Christ . . . the doctrinal fundamentals are not in dispute' (*Christian News-Letter*, July 1957, p. 32).

as the S.C.M. If only "Fundamentalists" would abandon their isolationism and come into these movements! They would lose nothing worth keeping; they would enrich the rest of the Church by sharing what God has taught them, and they would be enriched themselves as they learned what God has been teaching others. As it is, both sides are impoverished, and there is real danger that "fundamentalist" intransigence will end in schism.'

This is how some critics have analysed the situation. They are, in fact, only applying to this specific context things that during the past decade have been said again and again by ardent ecumenicals about 'Fundamentalists'. But the analysis is superficial and incorrect. It reflects two characteristic weaknesses of ecumenical theology. The first is the tendency to treat every theological tradition as no more than a loosely linked collection of isolated insights, brought together by the mere accident of history. But the evangelical faith is a systematic and integrated whole, built on a single foundation; and it must be understood and assessed as such. If, after recording their approval of the central themes of evangelical theology, these critics had looked below the surface and enquired into the foundation principle of that theology, they would not be able to say that they know of no major doctrinal issue separating the two sides. In fact, the cause of the division is, from one point of view, the deepest doctrinal divergence of all—disagreement as to the principle of authority; for there can be no stable agreement on anything between those who disagree here. Through treating the position of Evangelicals as mere bits and pieces and failing to ask why they believe the things that they do believe, the critics have missed this issue altogether. Yet it is the heart of the controversy, and it is here that our discussion must centre.

The second weakness of ecumenical thought which this analysis exposes is its conception of theological method. Its working principle is that all doctrinal views held, at any rate, by sizeable groups within Christendom are facets and fragments of God's truth, and should therefore be regarded as, in some way, complementary to each other. The way to construct a truly catholic theology is, accordingly, to conglomerate and, as far as possible, to fuse together all these different insights; and, where this cannot as yet be done, to hold them in tension till further analysis reveals the right way to combine them. And this programme, we are told, includes within its scope the insights of 'Fundamentalism', which are needed as much as any to make up the total picture.

We regard this conception as a half-truth; an important half-truth, certainly, but only a half-truth. And a half-truth treated as the whole truth becomes a complete untruth. We agree that no single human formulation of God's truth can be final or exhaustive; we agree that it will take the combined insight of the whole Church to grasp the whole truth of God, and that all groups within Christendom have much to learn from each other; we know that we are all prone to misunderstand the views of others, and to do so in an unfavourable sense; we recognize that there is at least a grain of truth in every heresy, and that views which are partly wrong are also partly right. It is indeed important in theological discussion to bear these things in mind. But it is even more important to remember that the essential step in sound theologizing is to bring all views—one's own as well as those of others—to the touchstone of Scripture. This is a step which much ecumenical theology seems to overlook. It tells us that older theology was woefully one-sided in its habit of treating opposing views simply as forms of error; but it is itself no less one-sided in its own habit of treating them simply as aspects of truth. Indeed, the last state is worse than the first; for the older theology, whatever its faults, was at least vividly conscious of the difference between truth and error, whereas the modern determination to judge the doctrinal disputes of Christendom as the Dodo judged the caucus-race ('*Everybody* has won, and all must have prizes') seems to show a degree of theological agnosticism and indifference to truth which is, to say the least, disturbing. The truth is that it is not enough to labour at assimilating the various views to each other. Such labour may serve to promote better mutual understanding; but we are not entitled to infer from the fact that a group of people are drawing nearer to each other that any of them is drawing nearer to the truth. Our first task must be to test all the words of men by the authoritative Word of God, to receive only what Scripture endorses, and to reject all that is contrary to it.[1] The essence of right theological method is thus reformation rather than conglomeration. For we may not assume in advance that all views are simply aspects of truth. Some of our fancied insights and cherished traditions may prove to be radical perversions of truth when tested by Scripture. We must take seriously what the Bible says about the reality of error in the Church (cf. Mt. vii. 15; 1 Tim. iv. 1 ff.; 1 Jn. iv. 1 ff.). So, when the Evangelical is assured by his critics that they do in fact approve of most of what he says and does, and is asked on that account to come and join them in further ecumenical enterprise, he declines. He thinks that the differences are being minimized and that the unity to which he is invited would prove a hollow pretence. Instead, the Evangelical asks his critics to come and join him in submitting the methods and conclusions of their respective theologies to the judgment of the written Word of God.

THE AIM OF THIS BOOK

In the following pages, we hope to do two things. First, we shall show what 'Fundamentalism' is. We have seen that it is widely interpreted as a modern movement of reaction. We shall show that, in fact, 'Fundamentalism' is just a twentieth-century name for historic Evangelicalism, though not, in our judgment, a very good or useful name. We shall show further that, although we must admit that many weaknesses and failings do manifest themselves, some of the oddities attributed to this movement are wholly imaginary, and that the rest are not the consequence of evangelical belief, but are rather inconsistencies which an Evangelicalism that is true to its own nature will be the first to deplore.

Then we shall discuss the fundamental question be-

[1] See Chapters III and IV below.

tween 'Fundamentalists' and their critics—the question of authority in the Christian Church. We shall show that authentic Christianity is a religion of biblical authority. In the course of our discussion, we shall see where some of the other issues raised in this controversy fit in. We shall deal, for instance, with the subject of biblical inerrancy, which Hebert regards (rightly in a sense, though not quite in the sense he supposes) as the heart of the evangelical position. He criticizes the concept of inerrancy as being negative;[1] but in fact, as we shall see, it is a very positive and significant notion, for it is basic to the doctrine of biblical authority. Only truth can be authoritative; only an inerrant Bible can be used, as we shall hope to show, in the way that God means Scripture to be used.

Again, we shall deal with the accusation of obscurantism. We have seen that some interpret this controversy as essentially an issue between the representatives of progress in biblical study and certain die-hard traditionalists who have set their faces against modern scholarship. We shall see that this is not so. Evangelicals do not wish to put the clock back to the days before scientific study began. What they desire is that modern Bible study should be genuinely scientific—that is to say, fully biblical in its method; and their chief complaint against modern criticism is that it so often fails here. It is true that Evangelicals call for a return to principles of Bible study which have a long history in the Christian Church, and for some revision of modern critical methods in the light of them. But that is not because these principles are traditional; it is because they are biblical. There is certainly an arrogant, hide-bound type of traditionalism, unthinking and uncritical, which is carnal and devilish. But there is also a respectful willingness to take help from the Church's past in order to understand the Bible in the present; and such traditionalism is spiritual and Christian. Moreover, it is this attitude alone that makes possible real progress in theology; for theology goes forward only by looking back —back through the Church's heritage of teaching to Jesus Christ and His apostles. Evangelicals seek to be tradi-

[1] *Op. cit.*, p. 42.

tionalists of this kind. If they lapse from the second kind of traditionalism to the first, they become bad Evangelicals, and their fall discredits not their principles, but themselves. No doubt there are bad Evangelicals; and the critics of 'Fundamentalism' have probably met them. Their false impressions may therefore be due simply to mistaking the nature of the genuine evangelical outlook. We shall say more of this later.

It may be helpful to outline the argument that we shall put forward in the following chapters. We shall maintain that Jesus Christ constituted Christianity a religion of biblical authority. He is the Church's Lord and Teacher; and He teaches His people by His Spirit through His written Word. As the Westminster Confession puts it: 'The supreme Judge, by which all controversies of religion are to be determined, and all decrees of councils, opinions of ancient writers, doctrines of men, and private spirits, are to be examined, and in whose sentence we are to rest, can be no other but the Holy Spirit speaking in the Scripture.'[1] We shall argue that subjection to the authority of Christ involves subjection to the authority of Scripture. Anything short of unconditional submission to Scripture, therefore, is a kind of impenitence; any view that subjects the written Word of God to the opinions and pronouncements of men involves unbelief and disloyalty towards Christ. Types of Christianity which regard as authoritative either tradition (as Romanism does) or reason (as Liberalism does) are perversions of the faith, for they locate the seat of authority, not in the Word of God, but in the words of men. Evangelicalism, however, seeking as it does to acknowledge in all things the supremacy of Scripture, is in principle Christianity at its purest and truest. We would not, indeed, deny that Evangelicals often fall below their principles, just as Roman Catholics and Liberal Protestants are themselves sometimes inconsistent and give to Scripture a position of authority which their principles would seem to disallow. Evangelicalism has no monopoly of gifts and graces. But that is not the point here. What we shall insist on is that the evangelical prin-

[1] I. x.

ciple of authority is authentically Christian, whereas other principles are not.

Accordingly, we shall contend that 'Fundamentalism' (in so far as consistent Evangelicalism is meant by this term) is in principle nothing but Christianity itself. The critics call it a new heresy. We shall give reasons for regarding it as the oldest orthodoxy, grounded four-square upon the teaching of Christ and His apostles. We are told that it is an eccentric deviation from the historic faith. We shall show that, in fact, it stands in the direct line of Christian development in a way that other forms of the faith do not. We are told that it is obscurantist, able to survive only by shutting its eyes to facts. We shall suggest that the boot is, in fact, on the other foot; that 'Fundamentalism' (again, consistent Evangelicalism is meant) has its eyes open to facts which its critics have not faced, and which are decisive against the positions which these latter occupy. It is said that 'Fundamentalists' have forfeited their intellectual honesty and are squandering the Church's intellectual heritage. We shall argue that, on the contrary, 'Fundamentalism' is the only consistently thought-out version of the faith, and the 'Fundamentalist' is the only Christian who uses his mind in a fully Christian way. It is said that 'Fundamentalism' narrows the mind. We shall see that what it really does is to set the mind free from current prejudice so that it can achieve a genuinely Christian outlook. 'Fundamentalists' are accused of spiritual pride. This is deplorable where it is true; but we shall suggest that, in fact, their doctrinal position expresses and inculcates intellectual humility. 'Fundamentalism' is said to be schismatic in spirit, and a threat to the unity of the Church; but we shall maintain that a consistent Evangelicalism is the truest catholicity. And we shall give reasons for thinking that the adverse judgments on 'Fundamentalism' which we have noted spring partly from failure to discern the nature of the thing judged and partly from failure to criticize the presuppositions on which those judgments rest. For we think that part of the reason, at least, why 'Fundamentalism' impresses its critics as distorted Christianity is that their own conception of Christianity is, in fact, distorted, and it is this, we believe, that more than anything else needs revision. Our critics wish that we would align ourselves with them. We look for a day when they will stand with us. For, wherever the terms 'heretical' and 'sectarian' may belong, they are out of place in the 'fundamentalist' camp. Consistent Evangelicals are the last Christians in the world to whom they apply.

CHAPTER II

WHAT IS 'FUNDAMENTALISM'?

'When I use a word,' Humpty Dumpty said in rather a scornful tone, 'it means just what I choose it to mean—neither more nor less.'

LEWIS CARROLL

IN this chapter we shall look into the history of the term 'Fundamentalism'. We have used it thus far as a synonym for Evangelicalism, because, whether the critics know it or not, it is Evangelicalism that they are attacking under this name. But the title is one which most British Evangelicals have always declined. Moreover, as we have seen, it is currently used in very varied senses. 'I am yet to meet two fundamentalists who can agree on an exact definition of fundamentalism,' wrote a correspondent in *The Times*; and the same must be said of anti-fundamentalists too. Remembering these facts, we must now try to decide whether the use of the word by either side in this debate is really helpful.

ORIGINS OF THE TERM

There is no mystery as to what the term meant when it was first coined. It was the title taken by a group of American Evangelicals, of all Protestant denominations, who banded themselves together to defend their faith against liberal encroachment after the First World War. The history of early Fundamentalism has been twice written, by S. G. Cole (*The History of Fundamentalism*, New York, 1931) and N. F. Furniss (*The Fundamentalist Controversy, 1918-31*, Yale, 1954).[1] It is instructive to see how the movement began. Since it arose as a protest against the type of Liberalism then current, we must first glance at that.

[1] See also 'The Word "Fundamentalist"' by Douglas Johnson in *The Christian Graduate*, March 1955, pp. 22 ff.

The clash between Liberalism and orthodox Evangelicalism during the first quarter of this century was sharper in America than in Britain. One reason for this was that American Evangelicalism had among its defenders men of a broader range of learning, deeper theological insight and greater intellectual virility than their British counterparts. Some of B. B. Warfield's polemical articles, and J. G. Machen's *Christianity and Liberalism*, for instance, crystallized the issues at stake in their broadest implications with a judicious mastery that cannot be too highly praised. A second reason was the more radical and uninhibited character of American Liberalism itself. The characteristic tenets of liberal faith in America in the early years of this century may be summarized as follows:[1]

1. God's character is one of pure benevolence—benevolence, that is, without standards. All men are His children, and sin separates no one from His love. The Fatherhood of God and the brotherhood of man are alike universal.

2. There is a divine spark in every man. All men, therefore, are good at heart, and need nothing more than encouragement to allow their natural goodness to express itself.

3. Jesus Christ is man's Saviour only in the sense that He is man's perfect Teacher and Example. We should regard Him simply as the first Christian, our elder brother in the world-wide family of God. He was not divine in any unique sense. He was God only in the sense that He was a perfectly God-conscious and God-guided man. He was not born of a virgin; He did not work miracles, in the sense of 'mighty works' of divine creative power; and He did not rise from the dead.

4. Just as Christ differs from other men only comparatively, not absolutely, so Christianity differs from other religions not generically, but merely as the best and highest type of religion that has yet appeared. All religions are

[1] We do not suggest that those who are opposing 'Fundamentalism' in the present debate all hold these particular views, or anything in detail like them. But we confess that we think it correct to describe their position as generically liberal for reasons which we shall give in their place in Chapter VII below.

forms of the same religion, just as all men are members of the same divine family. It follows, of course, that Foreign Missions should not aim to convert from one faith to another, but rather to promote a cross-fertilizing interchange whereby each religion may be enriched through the contribution of all others.

5. The Bible is not a divine record of revelation, but a human testament of religion; and Christian doctrine is not the God-given word which must create and control Christian experience. The truth is the opposite. Christian experience is directly infectious within the Christian community—it is 'caught', like mumps; and this experience creates and controls Christian doctrine, which is merely an attempt to give it verbal expression. Poetry, according to Wordsworth, consists of emotion recollected in tranquillity. Doctrine, according to Liberalism, has a precisely similar character. It is nothing more than an endeavour to put into words the content of religious feelings, impressions and intuitions. The only facts to which doctrinal statements give expression are the feelings of those who produce them. Doctrine is simply a by-product of religion. The New Testament contains the earliest attempts to express the Christian experience in words; its value lies in the fact that it is a first-hand witness to that experience. Other generations, however, must express the same experience in different words. Doctrinal formulæ, like poetic idiom, will vary from age to age and place to place, according to the variation of cultural backgrounds. The first-century theology of the New Testament cannot be normative for twentieth-century men. But this is no cause for concern, and means no loss. Doctrine is not basic or essential to any form of religion; no doctrinal statements or credal forms, therefore, are basic or essential to Christianity. In so far as there is a permanent and unchanging Christian message, it is not doctrinal, but ethical—the moral teaching of Jesus.

Not all Liberals went so far as this. But the views detailed above were all implicit in the liberal outlook, and some Liberals, at least, were ready to maintain them all. And, as Machen insisted, 'the true way in which to examine a spiritual movement is in its logical relations: logic is the great dynamic, and the logical implications of any way of thinking are sooner or later certain to be worked out'. His own *Christianity and Liberalism* was a demonstration that liberal views formed a coherent system—but one which was simply not Christian. The truth is that Liberalism was a deduction from the nineteenth-century view of 'religion' as a universal human phenomenon—a view which was itself of a piece with the characteristic nineteenth-century scientific and philosophical outlook. The faith of nineteenth-century science was that every phenomenon can be exactly classified and completely explained as an instance of some universal law of cause and effect; there are no unique events. The conviction of nineteenth-century philosophy, whether empiricist or idealist, materialist, deist or pantheist, was that the idea of supernatural interruptions of the course of the natural order was unphilosophical and absurd. Both science and philosophy relied on evolutionary concepts for the explanation of all things. Liberalism was an attempt to square Christianity with these anti-supernatural axioms. The result was tersely summed up by Machen: 'The liberal attempt at reconciling Christianity with modern science has really relinquished everything distinctive of Christianity, so that what remains is, in essentials, only that same indefinite type of religious aspiration which was in the world before Christianity came on the scene . . . the apologist has really abandoned what he started out to defend.'[1] Liberalism swept away entirely the gospel of the supernatural redemption of sinners by God's sovereign grace. It reduced grace to nature, divine revelation to human reflection, faith in Christ to following His example, and receiving new life to turning over a new leaf; it turned supernatural Christianity into one more form of natural religion, a thin mixture of morals and mysticism. As Hebert rightly says: 'Religion was being substituted for God.'[2] It was in protest against this radical refashioning of the historic faith that 'Fundamentalism' arose.

[1] *Christianity and Liberalism*, pp. 7 f.

[2] *Op. cit.*, p. 78.

The name developed out of the habit of referring to the central redemptive doctrines which Liberalism rejected as 'the fundamentals'. This usage goes back to at least 1909. In that year there appeared the first of twelve small miscellany volumes devoted to the exposition and defence of evangelical Christianity, entitled *The Fundamentals.* Through the generosity of two wealthy Californians, the set was sent free to 'every pastor, evangelist, missionary, theological student, Sunday School superintendent, Y.M.C.A. and Y.W.C.A. secretary in the English-speaking world, so far as the addresses of these can be obtained',[1] and over three million copies were eventually circulated. Among the authors who contributed to these volumes were men of the calibre of James Orr, B. B. Warfield, Sir Robert Anderson, H. C. G. Moule, W. H. Griffith Thomas, R. A. Torrey, Dyson Hague, A. T. Pierson and G. Campbell Morgan. Many of the articles were thoroughly scholarly pieces of work, as Hebert allows in his review of them.[2] The series contained positive biblical expositions of the controverted 'fundamentals'—the inspiration and authority of Scripture, the deity, virgin birth, supernatural miracles, atoning death, physical resurrection and personal return of Jesus Christ, the reality of sin, salvation by faith through spiritual regeneration, the power of prayer and the duty of evangelism. With these went polemics against positions opposed to the 'fundamentals'—Romanism, Darwinism, 'higher criticism' and such cults as Christian Science, Mormonism, Spiritualism and Jehovah's Witnesses—and some impressive personal testimonies to the power of Christ.

This use of 'the fundamentals' as a conservative slogan was echoed in the Deliverance which the General Assembly of the Northern Presbyterian Church issued in 1910, while *The Fundamentals* were in process of publication. This specified five items as 'the fundamentals of faith and of evangelical Christianity' : the inspiration and infallibility of Scripture, the deity of Christ, His virgin birth and miracles, His penal death for our sins, and His physical resurrection and personal return. From that time

[1] *The Fundamentals,* I. 4. [2] *Op. cit.,* pp. 17 ff.

on, it seems to have become habitual for American Evangelicals to refer to these articles as 'the fundamentals' simply. The General Assembly's list was adopted, with minor variations and additions, as the doctrinal platform of later 'fundamentalist' organizations, of which the first was the still surviving World Christian Fundamentals Association, formed in 1919. In 1920, a group of evangelical delegates to the Northern Baptist Convention held a preliminary meeting among themselves 'to re-state, re-affirm and re-emphasize the fundamentals of our New Testament faith'; whereupon an editorial in the Baptist *Watchman-Examiner* coined the title 'Fundamentalists' to denote 'those who mean to do battle royal for the fundamentals'. The word was at once taken up by both sides as a title for the defenders of the historic Christian position. The *Concise Oxford Dictionary* is thus right when it defines 'Fundamentalism' as : 'maintenance, in opposition to modernism, of traditional orthodox beliefs such as the inerrancy of Scripture and literal acceptance of the creeds as fundamentals of protestant Christianity.' This is what the term originally meant, and this is what the large number of American Evangelicals who still use it to describe their position mean by it today.

'FUNDAMENTALISM' AN OBJECTIONABLE TERM

Are British Evangelicals, then, 'Fundamentalists'? In the defined sense, they are; nor need they hesitate to admit it. It is no discredit to Christian men to be committed to the defence of 'the fundamentals'. But British Evangelicals are not 'Fundamentalists' in any of the other senses that have been put on the word. Nor have they ever adopted the name, or asked to be called by it; and sometimes they have explicitly rejected it. There are good reasons why they should continue to do so. To persons ignorant of the American debate about 'the fundamentals' (as most Englishmen are) the word can convey no obvious meaning. Its misuse in recent discussion makes it doubly unsuitable as a title. And there are three further reasons why British Evangelicals find it objectionable.

1. In the first place, it is a word that combines the vaguest conceptual meaning with the strongest emotional flavour. 'Fundamentalist' has long been a term of ecclesiastical abuse, a theological swear-word; and the important thing about a swear-word, of course, is not what it means but the feelings it expresses. It seems as discourteous as it is confusing to refer to Evangelicals as 'Fundamentalists' and so invoke against them all the contemptuous overtones that have gathered round the title. 'Give a dog a bad name—and hang it' is a time-honoured maxim in controversy—even, one fears, in theological controversy. And what happens once the 'bad name' has caught on is always the same : as its derogatory flavour grows stronger, it is used more and more widely and loosely as a general term of abuse, till it has lost all value as a meaningful description of anything.

This is the unchanging law of the vocabulary of insult. The history of some of the 'bad names' given to Evangelicals of other days yields instructive examples of it. 'Puritan', for instance, began as a rude name for Elizabethan Evangelicals who sought a more radical reformation and greater 'purity' in the worship and organization of the English Church. However, Thomas Fuller tells us, 'profane mouths quickly improved the nickname, therewith on every occasion to abuse pious people'.[1] Then, in the 1620s, the Laudian Arminians capitalized on its derogatory flavour when they drew attention from their own theological novelties by christening their opponents, the defenders of historic Anglican Calvinism, 'doctrinal Puritans'. Later, the word came to be thrown about in political and social contexts; any man of strict moral principles might be stigmatized by it; and 'puritanical' remains a potent insult to this day. As the word grew more derogatory, it was used more indiscriminately, and its original meaning fell wholly out of sight.

A similar example of the same thing is provided by the history of the word 'Methodist' in the eighteenth century. This title was first coined in 1730 as a sneering comment on the disciplined and methodical piety of John Wesley's

[1] *Church History of Britain*, 1837 ed., II, p. 474.

Oxford Holy Club. Then, it was applied generally to the members of Wesley's Societies. Thomas Scott tells us that by the end of the century 'Methodist, as a stigma of reproach . . . first applied to Mr. Wesley, Mr. Whitefield and their followers', had come to be a regular jibe against Anglican Evangelicals of all sorts ('all persons . . . who preach or profess the doctrines of the reformation, as expressed in the articles and liturgy of our church'). Scott goes on to illustrate by his own testimony how the psychology of prejudice operated against those to whom the word was applied. This is his description of his own attitude to 'Methodists' in the early years of his ministry: 'I joined in the prevailing sentiment; held them in sovereign contempt; spoke of them with derision; declaimed against them from the pulpit, as persons full of bigotry, enthusiasm and spiritual pride; laid heavy things to their charge; and endeavoured to prove the doctrine which I supposed them to hold (for I had never read their books) to be dishonourable to God and destructive to morality.'[1] Scott was so sure that it was a bad thing to be a Methodist that he did not take the trouble to enquire first-hand what Methodists really believed, but swallowed without hesitation all that was popularly said to their discredit. The anatomy of prejudice does not change. Put 'Fundamentalists' for 'Methodists', and one cannot help suspecting that Scott's confession is a cap that would fit some heads today.

There is no need to quote other examples; the point is clear. The verdict of history is that the use of vague prejudicial labels (and the more they are the one, the more they are the other) rules out the very possibility of charitable and constructive discussion. The interests of truth and love seem to demand that such labels be rigorously eschewed.

2. A further reason why British Evangelicals avoid calling themselves 'Fundamentalists' is that the name suggests Evangelicalism at something less than its best. American Fundamentalism did not in every respect adorn its doctrine. We honour the original Fundamentalists for their zeal to defend and spread their evangelical faith, but at a

[1] *The Force of Truth*, n.d., pp. 22 f.

generation's distance from them we can see serious limitations in the witness which they made. They were, by and large, outclassed by their opponents in learning and ability. Their original strategy had been directed towards regaining control of the established denominations, but they soon had to abandon all hope of that. As time went by, Fundamentalism withdrew more and more into the shell provided by its own inter-denominational organizations. Partly in self-defence, the movement developed a pronounced anti-intellectual bias; it grew distrustful of scholarship, sceptical as to the value of reasoning in matters of religion and truculent in its attitude towards the argument of its opponents. Something less than intellectual integrity appeared in its readiness to support a good cause with a bad argument. Its apologetics were makeshift, piecemeal and often unprincipled and unsound. Its adventures in the field of the natural sciences, especially with reference to evolution, were most unfortunate. Here, where the Fundamentalists' confidence was greatest, their competence was least, and their performance brought ridicule and discredit on themselves. Generally, Fundamentalism lacked theological energy and concern for Christian learning. It grew intellectually barren. Culture became suspect. The responsibilities of Christian social witness were left to the purveyors of the 'social gospel', and Fundamentalism turned it upon itself, limiting its interests to evangelism and the cultivation of personal religion. Neglecting Christian history, Fundamentalism lost touch with the past and left itself at the mercy of the present; the movement lacked depth and stability, and showed itself unduly susceptible to eccentric influences originating from its own ranks. The fundamentalist episode has not been a happy chapter in the history of Evengelicalism. The verdict of a modern American evangelical scholar, N. B. Stonehouse, on the movement as a whole is discerning and just: 'To the extent that fundamentalists were stressing the doctrines of the sovereignity of God as Creator and Ruler of the universe, the infallibility of the Scriptures, the deity of Christ and the reality of His incarnation, the supernaturalism of salvation, and the certainty of the coming consummation, they were simply defending historic Christianity. In this sense the fundamentalist-modernist controversy was but a phase of an age-long struggle. . . .

'On the other hand, though many modern critics are blameworthy for failing to distinguish within fundamentalism between the solid core of Biblical Christianity and certain excrescences, fundamentalists have often contributed to the judgment that it is essentially a religious novelty. The emergence of new emphases and the lack of others, the presence at times of a zeal not according to knowledge and the frequent absence of historical perspective and the appreciation of scholarship, have influenced this evaluation. . . . Oftentimes pietistic and perfectionist vagaries have come to be accepted as the hallmark of fundamentalism. And a one-sided other-worldliness, often associated with a dogmatic commitment to a futuristic chiliasm, has come to be widely regarded as essential to fundamentalist orthodoxy."[1]

We must not judge the original Fundamentalists too harshly. Their resources of scholarship were certainly limited, but their desire to defend the evangelical faith against a militant and aggressive Liberalism was equally certainly right. It was better to fight clumsily than not to fight at all. However, there is no doubt that their Evangelicalism was narrowed and impoverished by their controversial entanglements. Their Fundamentalism was Evangelicalism of a kind, but of a somewhat starved and stunted kind—shrivelled, coarsened and in part deformed under the strain of battle. To be true to its own nature as Evangelicalism, this fundamentalist tradition needs to be broadened, reformed and refined by the Word of God which it defends. It is the distinctive mark of Evangelicalism to keep itself loyal to Christ by constantly measuring, correcting and developing its faith and life by

[1] *J. Gresham Machen: A Biographical Memoir*, pp. 336 f. For a fuller discussion of Fundamentalism by an evangelical theologian, leading to similar conclusions, see Carl F. H. Henry, *Evangelical Responsibility in Contemporary Theology*, especially Chapter II (Eerdmans, 1957).

the standard of the Word of God. And Evangelicalism at its best has shown itself to be a much richer thing than this Fundamentalism which we have been describing : intellectually virile, church-centred in its outlook, vigorous in social and political enterprise and a cultural force of great power. The careers and achievements of such men as John Calvin, John Owen, John Wesley, Jonathan Edwards and Abraham Kuyper reflect something of the breadth of Evangelicalism when it is true to itself.

In particular, it is important to insist that obscurantism in all its forms is wholly out of keeping with true Evangelicalism. The Evangelical is not afraid of facts, for he knows that all facts are God's facts; nor is he afraid of thinking, for he knows that all truth is God's truth, and right reason cannot endanger sound faith. He is called to love God with all his mind; and part of what this means is that, when confronted by those who, on professedly rational grounds, take exception to historic Christianity, he must set himself not merely to deplore or denounce them, but to out-think them. It is not his business to argue men into faith, for that cannot be done; but it is his business to demonstrate the intellectual adequacy of the biblical faith and the comparative inadequacy of its rivals, and to show the invalidity of the criticisms that are brought against it. This he seeks to do, not from any motive of intellectual self-justification, but for the glory of God and of His gospel. A confident intellectualism expressive of robust faith in God, whose Word is truth, is part of the historic evangelical tradition. If present-day Evangelicals fall short of this, they are false to their own principles and heritage.[1]

Few men of recent years have so vigorously expressed their belief in the rational superiority of Evangelicalism over its modern rivals as the late J. G. Machen, who died in 1937. Machen was, in Furniss' phrase, 'a strange bedfellow for most Fundamentalists'[2] by reason of the purity of his Evangelicalism at this point. Liberalism, then as now, affirmed that to maintain evangelical orthodoxy in

[1] See also Chapters V and VI.

[2] *The Fundamentalist Controversy, 1918–31*, pp. 127 f.

the twentieth century was intellectually retrograde and, in effect, dishonest. Machen's reply was that it was in fact the liberal position that was open to this kind of criticism. Liberal thinking, he maintained, is really superficial, and can be shown to be so; and the true remedy against Liberalism is for men to think, not less (as some Fundamentalists seemed to suppose) but more—more deeply, more vigorously, more clearly and more critically.[1] Paradoxically, but, we believe, correctly, Machen analysed the basic cause of the present eclipse of Evangelicalism as the radically anti-intellectual outlook of the twentieth century. The very quantity of books to read and facts to master with which the twentieth-century man is confronted encourages him to think broadly and superficially about much, but hinders him from thinking deeply and thoroughly about anything. Some words which Machen wrote on this subject in 1925 seem so apt today that we quote them at length:

'It is a great mistake . . . to suppose that we who are called "conservatives" hold desperately to certain beliefs merely because they are old, and are opposed to the discovery of new facts. On the contrary, we welcome new discoveries with all our hearts, and we believe that our cause will come to its rights again only when youth throws off its present intellectual lethargy, refuses to go thoughtlessly with the anti-intellectual current of the age, and recovers some genuine independence of mind. In one sense, indeed, we are traditionalists. . . . But on the whole, in view of the conditions that now exist, it would perhaps be more correct to call us "radicals" than to call us "conservatives". . . . We are seeking in particular to arouse youth from its present uncritical repetition of current phrases into some genuine examination of the basis of life; and we believe that Christianity flourishes not in the darkness, but in the light. A revival of the Christian religion, we believe, will deliver mankind from its present bondage. Such a revival will not be the work of man, but the work

[1] Machen himself showed how this might be done in two masterly critical studies, *The Origin of Paul's Religion* (1921) and *The Virgin Birth of Christ* (1930).

of the Spirit of God. But one of the means which the Spirit will use, we believe, is an awakening of the intellect. . . . The new Reformation, in other words, will be accompanied by a new Renaissance; and the last thing in the world that we desire to do is to discourage originality or independence of mind."[1]

Machen, with his robust Christian intellectualism, his demand for a scholarly apologetic, and his strong churchmanship, did not like being called a 'Fundamentalist'. In truth, as Dr. Stonehouse points out, 'judged by various criteria adopted by friend and foe, he was not a fundamentalist at all'.[2] He saw Fundamentalism as a debased Evangelicalism which at point after point was at variance with that for which he stood. British Evangelicals do not like to be called 'Fundamentalists' either, and for a similar reason.

It would not be right to leave this point without a frank acknowledgment that Evangelicals in this country have on occasion reproduced some of those features of 'Fundamentalism' which Machen most regretted—distrust of reason, shoddy apologetics, cultural barrenness, eccentric individualism, indifference to churchmanship. The conflict with a self-confident Liberalism had similar effects on both sides of the Atlantic. British Evangelicals also have been heard sneering at 'the critics', making a virtue of theological ignorance, belittling scholarship and opposing 'reason' to 'simple faith' in such a way as to suggest that the purest version of Christianity is that which takes least thought to grasp. Here, also, fear has on occasion masqueraded as faith. One reason why Evangelicals are regarded by some as obscurantist is that, in fact, they sometimes are. The fault is real; we shall do well to humble ourselves because of it.

On the other hand, however, it would equally not be right to leave this point without emphasizing once more that the fundamentalist rejection of Liberalism expressed, not a mere natural human reluctance to abandon an old thing, but a God-given spiritual insight into the character

[1] *What is Faith?*, pp. 17 f.

[2] *J. Gresham Machen: A Biographical Memoir*, p. 337.

of the new thing. Liberalism maintained that modern literary and historical criticism had exploded the doctrine of an infallible Bible, modern science had made it impossible to believe in the supernatural as Scripture presents it, modern comparative study of religions had shown that Christianity, after all, was not unique, and modern philosophy required the dismissal of such basic biblical concepts as original sin, the wrath of God and expiatory sacrifice, as primitive superstitions. Against each of these positions sensitive Christian consciences protested, as they always will. Each position involves a denial of the apostolic gospel; and therefore Christian consciences sense at once that they are false, even before it is clear what in detail is wrong with them. John spoke of the Christian's God-given capacity to discern denials of the gospel for what they are when he wrote : 'Ye have an unction from the Holy One, and ye know all things' (1 Jn. ii. 20; cf. verses 26, 27).[1] God's Spirit will not witness to a repudiation of God's Word or a perversion of Christ's gospel. Those Evangelicals who reacted against Liberalism so violently as to repudiate the use of reason in religion altogether were certainly wrong; the antidote for bad reasoning is not no reasoning, but better reasoning. But in that they did react, they were just as certainly right. A sound spiritual instinct guided them, and we should thank God for the tenacity with which they held their ground.

For it required tenacity on their part. In their day, Liberalism was dominant; the evolutionary outlook of which it was a product was well-nigh universal, and the nineteenth-century faith that mankind was progressing towards perfection, in religion as in all else, was still unchallenged. From that point of view, it was harder then to hold to the biblical faith than it is now. The events of the past thirty years have shaken evolutionary optimism to its foundation. The supernaturalism of the Bible does not now seem such an anachronism as does the evolutionary outlook which once claimed to supersede it. The thought of divine wrath and judgment is less incredible after

[1] The RV margin and RSV read 'and ye all know', perhaps rightly; but this does not affect our point.

two world wars. The idea that man is so radically bad that only a divine Saviour can help him no longer seems self-evidently absurd. Liberalism itself is not dead; but the older form of it is largely extinct, and the trend of modern theology, on the whole, is back towards the historic faith rather than away from it. Evangelical faith today does not involve such a complete break with the prevalent mood of the Church as it did in the complacent days when Fundamentalism arose. We honour Fundamentalism for its witness at a time when a militant Liberalism threatened to sweep the historic faith away. But we honour it best, not by perpetuating its weaknesses, but by frankly acknowledging them and taking pains to avoid them. The way for us to show gratitude to God for the courageous battle which the Fundamentalists fought is by seeking to reopen the richer vein of the Evangelicalism which they laboured to defend. And therefore we prefer to call ourselves 'Evangelicals' rather than 'Fundamentalists'.

3. The final reason why Evangelicals decline to be called 'Fundamentalists' is that the term is modern. Its meaning derives from a modern controversy, and its very formation suggests that what it describes is just one 'ism' among the many that our age has bred. But Evangelicalism is precisely not that. It is, we maintain, the oldest version of Christianity; theologically regarded, it is just apostolic Christianity itself. Ideally, the Evangelical would choose no title for himself but 'Christian'. He holds that he alone is entitled to call his faith 'Christian' without qualification. If, however, he must use a further label to differentiate himself from other groups within the Church, he accepts 'Evangelical' as being the historically established term for his position, and one which by its very form bears witness to his belief that, of all forms of Christianity, this alone is loyal to the nature and content of the Evangel. It is common today to prefix 'conservative' to the traditional title in order to mark off Evangelicalism of the older sort from the so-called 'liberal evangelical' position. But if the term 'Evangelicalism' be given its historic meaning—fidelity to the doctrinal content of the gospel—then 'liberal Evangelicalism' is a contradiction in terms, and

the movement which goes by that name should be called 'pietistic Liberalism', or something of the sort. Logically, 'conservative' is superfluous; 'Evangelical' says all that is meant.

When the Evangelical identifies his faith with apostolic Christianity, he does not mean that he regards as unimportant, or wishes to ignore, the theological legacy of the past nineteen centuries of the Church's life. He recognizes that, through the guiding activity of the Holy Spirit who indwells the Church to lead it into truth, there has been a legitimate and necessary advance in elucidating the contents and plumbing the depths of the revelation which God once for all delivered to the saints and deposited in the Scriptures. The Evangelical will value the work of the Fathers in defining the doctrines of the Trinity and incarnation, of Anselm and the Reformers in drawing out the doctrine of atonement, of Luther in expounding justification by faith, of Calvin and the Puritans in tracing out the work of the Holy Spirit, and of all others, past and present, who have contributed to the Church's doctrinal heritage. He will acknowledge also that the Church now sees further into the political and social implications of the gospel than it did at the beginning, having been repeatedly forced to re-examine these implications as society has grown more complex. But he insists that this whole process of growth in understanding, which still goes on, must be controlled and judged by that very Word of God which it seeks to elucidate, so as to ensure that it serves simply to display, and not in any way to alter, the distinctive doctrines of Christianity. And it is here, he thinks, that the various sorts of 'Catholicism', on the one hand, and of liberal Protestantism, on the other, are found wanting. In the course of the development which produced them, they have to a greater or less degree become something other than Christianity. They are the eccentricities and novelties, while Evangelicalism alone stands in the true line of Christian development.

The predominance of Liberalism during the past half-century has led to the present paradoxical state of affairs —that Evangelicalism, which is really old, is now so unfamiliar that men treat it as more of a novelty than what is really new. Our critics suppose that what they call 'Fundamentalism' is something as new as its name. But it is not. Nor was sixteenth-century Protestantism, nor seventeenth-century Puritanism, nor eighteenth-century Methodism. These names denote simply particular aspects and episodes of the continuing history of evangelical Christianity—Christianity according to Jesus Christ and His apostles. 'Fundamentalism' is a recent chapter in that history, now closing, if not already closed. The chapters end, but the history goes on. The idea that the present-day evangelical movement is essentially a novelty in the Church is a complete illusion; and it is a vital part of the present-day defence of Evangelicalism to destroy that illusion. But for Evangelicals to accept a new name—whether 'Fundamentalism' or any other—could only serve to foster it. Therefore they decline new names. They prefer to call attention to their spiritual ancestry and the claim which they make for their faith by adhering to the historic title for it.

Of another 'ism' much discussed in the Church today, Canon Roger Lloyd has written : 'The introduction of the word . . . has been the signal for clear thinking to fly out of the window. . . . All words must be dubious when you have laboriously to explain what you do not mean by them. It might be a good idea to give them up for Lent.' This is exactly what we would say of 'Fundamentalism'. The word is prejudicial, ambiguous, explosive and in every way unhelpful to discussion. It does not clarify; it merely confuses. It is only in use today because critics of Evangelicalism have dragged it up. For the rest of our argument we shall abandon it, and speak of Evangelicalism simply. We would plead that in future others will do the same.

CHAPTER III

AUTHORITY

My conscience is subject to the Word of God.

MARTIN LUTHER

The authority of the holy scripture, for which it ought to be believed and obeyed, dependeth not upon the testimony of any man or church, but wholly upon God (who is truth itself), the author thereof; and therefore it is to be received, because it is the word of God.

WESTMINSTER CONFESSION, I. IV

THE PROBLEM STATED

WE have said already that one odd feature of this controversy is that the real question, or group of questions, that lies at its heart has not yet been raised. The real question concerns the principle of authority. But anti-fundamentalists fail to see this. Hence, instead of recognizing and discussing the difference that exists here, we find them glossing over it with equivocal formulæ. Hebert, for instance, more than once affirms the authority of God's word, of the gospel, of Christ, in terms which Evangelicals would use. But his book shows that he does not mean them in an evangelical sense. Yet he seems quite unaware that there is any difference of view at this point, and supposes that disagreement begins only over principles of biblical interpretation. This is typical of those who write and speak against Evangelicalism today. What they say reveals that, in the strict sense of the phrase, many of them do not know what they are talking about.

In the following chapters we address ourselves to this situation. Our aim is to clarify the neglected issues. We shall try to formulate the question of authority, specify the difference of the contending groups about it, and justify our claim that it is central in the present dispute. We shall expound the evangelical view, and work out its implications; and we hope to do this in enough detail to remove the possibility of further confusion arising through the use of the ambiguous formulæ now in vogue. This will involve us in a critique of some common views, and of the anti-fundamentalist outlook as a whole. We hope to make clear the implications of the position that opposes our own, and to confirm our argument for the rightness of the one by exhibiting the wrongness of the other. What we shall write is not offered as in any sense an exhaustive statement; our aim is limited to saying what seems necessary in order to make clear the basic issues in this debate and the foundations of the evangelical position. We shall confine ourselves as far as possible to broad principles; many points of detail must be passed by for lack of space. As it is, the aim which we have set ourselves will involve us in fairly full discussions.

We would begin this chapter by calling attention to the extreme importance of its subject.

The problem of authority is the most fundamental problem that the Christian Church ever faces. This is because Christianity is built on truth : that is to say, on the content of a divine revelation. Christianity announces salvation through faith in Jesus Christ, in and through whom that revelation came to completion; but faith in Jesus Christ is possible only where the truth concerning Him is known. The New Testament tells us that God has made provision for the communication of this saving truth. He entrusted to the apostles, and through them to the whole Church, a message from Himself which conveys it. This is called 'the word of God', 'the word of the Lord', or sometimes 'the word' simply.[1] Its contents denominate it 'the word of Christ', 'the word of the cross';[2] and its divine origin guarantees it to be 'the word of truth'.[3] Men come to faith through receiving this word, and such faith is specifically described as 'obeying the truth'.[4] 'The faith of

[1] Acts iv. 31, vi. 2, viii. 4, 14; Col. i. 25; 1 Thes. i. 8, ii. 13, etc.
[2] Col. iii. 16; 1 Cor. i. 18, RV.
[3] 2 Cor. vi. 7; Col. i. 5; Eph. i. 13; 2 Tim. ii. 15; Jas. i. 18.
[4] Gal. iii. 1, v. 7; 1 Pet. i. 22; cf. Rom. vi. 17, x. 16; 2 Thes. i. 8; 1 Pet. iv. 17.

God's elect' goes with 'the knowledge of the truth'.[1] But if this truth is rejected or perverted, faith is overthrown (cf. 2 Tim. ii. 18) and men come under the power of a lie (cf. 2 Thes. ii. 10-13), with terrible results. The startlingly violent tone of Paul's Epistle to the Galatians reflects his vivid awareness of this. The circumcision heresy might seem a small thing in itself, but Paul knew that revealed truth was all of a piece, and that to follow out the principle which this heresy enshrined would mean the effective abandonment of the gospel; so he writes: 'Behold, I Paul say unto you, that, if ye receive circumcision, Christ will profit you nothing. . . . Ye are severed from Christ . . . ye are fallen away from grace.'[2] Hence the vehemence of his twice-repeated imprecation: 'Though we, or an angel from heaven, should preach unto you any gospel other than that which we preached unto you, let him be anathema. As we have said before, so say I now again, If any man preacheth unto you any gospel other than that which ye received, let him be anathema.'[3] Paul finds himself unable to over-estimate the importance of holding fast the truth and avoiding error as to the content of the gospel. Here he is in line with the witness of the whole New Testament. Modern man, sceptical and indifferent as he is to dogmatic pronouncements about the supernatural order, may find it hard to take seriously the idea that one's eternal welfare may depend on what one believes; but the apostles were sure that it was so. Theological error was to them a grim reality, as was the spiritual shipwreck which comes in its wake.

Hence we see how important it is to find a right criterion of truth, by which we may tell the word of God from human error. The New Testament tells us that 'many false prophets are gone out into the world',[4] and holds out no hope that the world will ever be without them. We must expect to find error constantly assailing the truth; Christendom will always be a theological battlefield. But in that case the Christian's most pressing need in every age

[1] Tit. i. 1, RV. [2] Gal. v. 2–4, RV.
[3] Gal. i. 8, 9, RV. [4] 1 Jn. iv. 1; cf. 2 Jn. 7.

is to have a reliable principle by which he may test the conflicting voices that claim to speak for Christianity and so make out amid their discordant clamour what he ought to believe and do.

Here, however, difficulty arises, for several possible principles present themselves. In the imprecatory passage quoted from the Galatians, for instance, Paul is specifically warning against one plausible but unreliable criterion—the personal dignity of the speaker. The New Testament knows of others. Paul cautions Timothy against treating as a criterion 'the profane babblings and oppositions of the knowledge (*gnōsis,* the current religious philosophy) which is falsely so called; which some professing have erred concerning the faith'.[1] We are also told that teaching may have the status of honoured tradition, or be the product of exalted, visionary states of mind, and yet not be true;[2] so that these factors provide no safe criterion. Yet we find that all these principles of authority which the New Testament rejects have, in fact, had a long history within the Christian Church.

This being so, we must not be surprised that the problem of authority still divides Christian people. And clearly it is the most far-reaching and fundamental division that there is, or can be, between them. The deepest cleavages in Christendom are doctrinal; and the deepest doctrinal cleavages are those which result from disagreement about authority. Radical divergences are only to be expected when there is no agreement as to the proper grounds for believing anything. The doctrinal divisions in the Church therefore fall into two distinct classes. Some presuppose a common view of authority; some do not. The seventeenth-century debates between Presbyterians and Independents, or Calvinists and Arminians, were examples of the first class; in them, both sides agreed that Scripture is the final authority and differed only as to what it teaches. On the other hand, the historic differences between Protestantism and Rome over the Papacy, the priesthood and the Mass belong to the second

[1] 1 Tim. vi. 20, 21, RV.
[2] Mk. vii. 6–13; Col. ii. 18; see below, pp. 49 ff.

class; for these divisions reflect the fact that the disputants are divided about authority. Plainly, these two classes of disagreement must be approached at different levels. Any plan for settling the doctrinal disputes of Christendom which overlooked the distinction between them, and tried to resolve disagreements of the second type as if they were of the first—to settle them, in other words, without raising the question of authority at all—would stand condemned as quite unrealistic and misguided. Those who disagree as to the principle of authority and, in consequence, as to the right method in theology, can reach no significant agreement on anything else.

It is, however, a disturbing fact that today this is largely overlooked. Christian bodies of all sorts are constantly urged to come together, sink their differences and present a united front to the forces of secularism and Communism. It is taken for granted that the differences in question are small and trifling—unsightly little cracks on the surface of an otherwise solid wall. But this assumption is false. Not all the cracks are mere superficial disfigurements; some of them are the outward signs of lack of structural integration. The wall is cracked because it is not all built on the same foundation. The more one probes the differences between Roman and Protestant, Liberal and Evangelical, the deeper they prove to be; beneath the cracks on the surface lie fissures which run down to the very foundations, broadening as they go. Nothing is gained just by trying to cement up the cracks; that only encourages the collapse of the entire wall. Sham unity is not worth working for, and real unity, that fellowship of love in the truth which Christ prayed that His disciples might enjoy,[1] will come only as those sections of the wall which rest on unsound foundations are dismantled and rebuilt. Till this happens, the question of authority must remain central in discussion between the dissident groups; and the best service one can do to the divided Church of Christ is to keep it there.

We maintain that the 'fundamentalist' controversy is of the second type mentioned; that is, that it is rooted in disagreement about authority. It is, in fact, an episode

[1] Jn. xvii. 17–23.

in the continuing debate between Evangelicalism and what we shall call Subjectivism, of which Liberalism is a modern form. And it is idle to hope that we and our critics can reach stable agreement on other matters while we lack common ground on the subject of authority. This is the contention which we shall now expound.

The problem of authority may be formulated thus. All Christians agree that Christianity, being founded on revelation, is a religion of authority, requiring that its adherents conform themselves to the revelation on which it rests. This revelation was given in history, in the course of a process of redemptive action which centred upon the life, death and resurrection of Jesus Christ. Authority derives from this revelation. What God says to man and does for man in the present is no more than a particular application of what He said to the world and did for the world once for all through the man Christ Jesus. It is God speaking in Christ, and God's word spoken through Christ, that is ultimately authoritative; it is the Bible that bears authoritative witness to the speaking of that word; and it is the Holy Spirit who, in every age, mediates that authoritative word to the individual Christian and the Church. These general conceptions are common ground. The problem arises when we try to be more specific and practical in our forms of statement. How should we set about discovering just what this word of God is? By what channel exactly is it mediated from the past to the present? From what source may we gain authoritative guidance as to what God has and has not authoritatively said? When Christian opinions differ, where should be the final court of appeal? This is the problem of authority.

THREE RIVAL ANSWERS

There are three distinct authorities to which final appeal might be made—Holy Scripture, Church tradition or Christian reason; that is to say, Scripture as interpreted by itself; Scripture as interpreted (and in some measure amplified) by official ecclesiastical sources; and Scripture as evaluated in terms of extra-biblical principles by individual Christian men. The problem of authority can be answered in three ways, and three only, according to which of the authorities mentioned is given precedence over the other two: we call these three types of answer the evangelical, the traditionalist and the subjectivist respectively. Confessional Protestants give the first; Romanists, some Anglo-Catholics and Orthodox give the second; modern Liberal Protestants give the third. The consequent threefold division of Christendom on the subject of authority cuts across many denominational barriers, and is in fact the deepest cleavage of all.

We must briefly set out these three positions side by side. Analysed in terms of principle, they are as follows:

a. The Evangelical View

This was first formally stated in opposition to the other two at the time of the Reformation, but, as we shall see, it is in fact the original Christian position. Its basic principle is that the teaching of the written Scriptures is the Word which God spoke and speaks to His Church, and is finally authoritative for faith and life. To learn the mind of God, one must consult His written Word. What Scripture says, God says. The Bible is inspired in the sense of being word-for-word God-given. It is a record and explanation of divine revelation which is both complete (*sufficient*) and comprehensible (*perspicuous*); that is to say, it contains all that the Church needs to know in this world for its guidance in the way of salvation and service, and it contains the principles for its own interpretation within itself. Furthermore, the Holy Spirit, who caused it to be written, has been given to the Church to cause believers to recognize it for the divine Word that it is, and to enable them to interpret it rightly and understand its meaning. He who was its Author is also its Witness and Expositor. Christians must therefore seek to be helped and taught by the Spirit when they study Scripture, and must regard all their understanding of it, no less than the book itself, as the gift of God. The Spirit must be acknowledged as the infallible Interpreter of God's infallible Word. 'The supreme Judge . . . in whose sentence we are to rest, can be no other but the Holy Spirit speaking in the Scripture.'[1]

The Bible, therefore, does not need to be supplemented and interpreted by tradition, or revised and corrected by reason. Instead, it demands to sit in judgment on the dictates of both; for the words of men must be tried by the Word of God. The Church collectively, and the Christian individually, can and do err, and the inerrant Scripture must ever be allowed to speak and correct them.

Not that Church tradition is unimportant. On the contrary, it yields much valuable help in understanding what Scripture teaches. The Spirit has been active in the Church from the first, doing the work He was sent to do —guiding God's people into an understanding of revealed truth. The history of the Church's labour to understand the Bible forms a commentary on the Bible which we cannot despise or ignore without dishonouring the Holy Ghost. To treat the principle of biblical authority as a prohibition against reading and learning from the book of Church history is not an evangelical, but an anabaptist mistake, which comes from overlooking what the Bible says of the Spirit's work in the Church. Tradition may not be so lightly dismissed. But neither may it be made a separate authority apart from Scripture. Like every commentary on the Bible, it must itself be tested and, where necessary, corrected by the Bible which it seeks to expound.

Nor may reason be viewed as an independent authority for our knowledge of God's truth. Reason's part is to act as the servant of the written Word, seeking in dependence on the Spirit to interpret Scripture scripturally, to correlate its teaching and to discern its application to all parts of life. We may not look to reason to tell us whether Scripture is right in what it says (reason is not in any case competent to pass such a judgment); instead, we must look to Scripture to tell us whether reason is right in what it thinks on the subjects with which Scripture deals.

On this view, then, the proper ground for believing a thing is not that the Church or reason says it. Both these

[1] Westminster Confession, I. x.

authorities may err, and in any case it is not to them that God has told us to go for authoritative indications of His mind. The proper ground for believing a thing is that God says it in His written Word, and a readiness to take God's word and accept what He asserts in the Bible is thus fundamental to faith.

b. The Traditionalist View

This deviates from that expounded above towards an ecclesiastical authoritarianism. It maintains that the final authority for faith and life is the official teaching of the institutional Church. To learn the mind of God, one should consult the Church's historic tradition; what the Church says, God says. (The fact that 'Catholic' bodies differ as to the limits of tradition does not affect their unity on this principle.) This view does not question that the Bible is God-given and therefore authoritative; but it insists that Scripture is neither *sufficient* nor *perspicuous*, neither self-contained nor self-interpreting, as an account of God's revelation. The Bible alone, therefore, is no safe nor adequate guide for anyone. However, tradition, which is also God-given and therefore authoritative, supplies what is lacking in Scripture; it augments its contents and declares its (alleged) meaning. (Rome goes furthest in thus supplementing and wresting Scripture, adding the Apocrypha to the canon, treating the Vulgate as an authentic version, and imposing such traditions as Papal infallibility and the Mary-cult; others are less extravagant.) The work of the Holy Spirit as Giver and Interpreter of revelation is thus equated with the pronouncements of the teaching Church. This view allows reason no authority to judge tradition; reason's task is to receive, record and apply tradition, not to test it. The practical implication of this position is that the reason why a Christian should believe a thing is not that he sees for himself that the Bible says it (though it may), nor that his reason approves it (it may, or it may not), but that the Church teaches it. Faith is primarily a matter of believing what the Church lays down.

c. The Subjectivist Position

This is a veritable chameleon, and takes many forms. Sometimes it appears as mysticism (as in the Quakers), sometimes as rationalism (as in the Socinians and Deists), sometimes as a combination of both (as in some nineteenth-century Liberals who took their mysticism from Schleiermacher and their rationalism from Ritschl). But all its many varieties spring from a single principle, namely, that the final authority for my faith and life is the verdict of my reason, conscience or religious sentiment (subjectivists vary in the way they put this) as I examine Scripture 'with an open mind' (i.e., without presupposing that its own account of itself is true), and measure it by what I have learned from other sources, historical, philosophical, religious and scientific. What under these circumstances reason and conscience say, what I find that 'I feel', that God says.

In general, the subjectivism of the past century has given some such account of the Bible as this : Scripture is certainly a product of outstanding religious insight. God was with its authors. They were inspired to write, and what they wrote is inspiring to read. But their inspiration was not of such a kind as to guarantee the full truth of their writings, or to make them all the word of God. Like all human products, Scripture is uneven. One part contradicts another; some parts are uninspired and unimportant; some of it reflects an antiquated outlook which can have no relevance for today. (The same, of course, on this view is true of Church tradition.) If the essential biblical message is to mean anything to modern man, it must be divorced from its obsolete trappings, re-formulated in the light of modern knowledge and re-stated in terms drawn from the thought-world of today. Reason and conscience must judge Scripture and tradition, picking out the wheat from the chaff and re-fashioning the whole to bring it into line with the accepted philosophy of the time. The work of the Spirit as interpreter is equated with this endless activity of reconstruction. According to subjectivism, therefore, the proper ground for believing a thing is not that the Bible or tradition contains it, but that reason and conscience commend it; from which it seems to follow that faith is essentially a matter of being loyal to such religious convictions as one has.

Here, then, are the three rival answers to the problem of authority. They are mutually exclusive, and cannot in reality be combined. Sometimes, it is true, an attempt is made to combine them in a formula, and we are told that Scripture, tradition and reason should be regarded as co-ordinate authorities, neither being set above the other two. But the formula is unworkable; what happens when they clash? There seems no other way of making sense of the formula than to suppose that it conceals an intention of accepting all that Scripture and tradition are held to agree upon, but of appealing to the arbitration of reason when they differ. If so, then, of course, reason is the ultimate authority all along; neither Scripture nor tradition is to be followed further than reason approves. The formula thus enshrines one of the many forms of subjectivism, and is not a fourth option at all. There is no fourth option.

Which of these three, now, is the authentic Christian position? That is what we have to decide.

THE NEW TESTAMENT IN RELATION TO THE OLD

It is convenient in the first instance to approach this as an historical question, to be answered by appeal to historical matter of fact. Christianity is an historical religion, and had an historical Founder, whose teaching all Christians profess to regard as normative. The authentic Christian position on any subject, therefore, will be that which corresponds with what He taught. The New Testament, regarded simply as an historical document, provides us with first-hand contemporary evidence as to what the earliest Christians held that Christ had taught, and accordingly, as to what they believed themselves. Whether the teaching of the New Testament, on this or any other subject, is to be treated as final is a question which for the moment we postpone, though the answer to it will become clear as we go along. For the moment, we simply ask: What, in fact, is the New Testament position on authority?

The entire New Testament outlook is determined by the conviction that the Old and New dispensations are organically one. The writers see the coming of Christ as the climax of a single revelatory process which had been going on in Israel for over a millennium; and their writings, in which this crowning revelation is described and explained, ask to be read as the complement and completion of the Old Testament. Whether or not they knew that any part of what they wrote was designed by God for canonical Scripture, none of them doubted the essential continuity between what they were saying and what the Scriptures of the Old Covenant said. To them, the Old and the New were all of a piece; the contents of the New had been concealed in the Old, and the meaning of the Old stood revealed in the New. Christianity was no fresh start, but the finishing of something begun long before.

Both Christ and the apostles were at pains to insist that, revolutionary though the new order might seem, it was in fact no more than had been foretold when the prophets spoke of the coming of Israel's Messiah and the setting up of His kingdom. This theme constantly recurs in the early Christian preaching.[1] Christ had already made the point that the relation between the new order and the old was one not of mere substitution, but of fulfilment. 'Think not that I am come to destroy the law, or the prophets: I am not come to destroy, but to fulfil.'[2] The consequence of His coming was that the life of the Church of God was reconstructed in its permanent and final form. As a result, the Church came to look very different from what it had been before. It became a mainly Gentile body, in which most Jews had no place. It lost its national life and became an international society. Its characteristic rites were no longer circumcision and the annual passover, but baptism and the weekly Lord's Supper; and whereas the synagogue had met on the seventh day, Christians came together on the first day of the week. They had no priestly

[1] Cf. Acts ii. 16 ff., iii. 18 ff., x. 43, xiii. 32 ff., etc.

[2] Mt. v. 17.

caste nor central shrine: they offered no animal sacrifices. They had abandoned all the elaborate Old Testament machinery for bringing sinners near to a holy God; they claimed that it had been done away by the Messiah's priestly sacrifice of Himself, which won permanent access to God for all believers everywhere. The outward differences between the Old and the New order were thus considerable; yet the apostles insisted that the Christian community was essentially the same Church as before. Gentile converts were told that in Christ they had become 'the Israel of God', 'Abraham's seed' and heirs of the Abrahamic promise, for they had now been grafted into the one olive tree (the covenant community, of which the patriarchs were the root and first-fruits) in place of those of Abraham's lineal seed who were broken off through unbelief.[1] The God of the Christians was the God of Israel; Jesus, the Son of God, was the Christ, Israel's long-awaited Messiah; and Christianity itself was no more than Israel's religion brought to its perfect and final form through the fulfilment of Israel's hope by Christ's death and resurrection.

In the light of this professed continuity between the old and the new dispensations it is very significant for our enquiry to find that Israel's religion had always been based on the authority of a written word of God. It was on record that when God first entered into covenant with the nation at Sinai and gave them His laws, He inscribed the Decalogue—the core of the code—on two tables of stone, 'written with the finger of God', which Moses brought down from the mountain and deposited in the Ark.[2] The biblical concept of written revelation seems to have been directly derived from those tables. The rest of the Pentateuch, and the later prophetic messages, written down either by the prophets themselves[3] or by their associates,[4] were always regarded as no less divine, no less truly words of God, than the words which God had written with His own finger. The fact of their human authorship was never

[1] Gal. iii. 29, vi. 16; cf. Rom. iv. 11 ff., xi. 17 ff.
[2] Ex. xxxi. 18; Dt. iv. 13, x. 5.
[3] Cf. Hab. ii. 2.
[4] Cf. Je. xxxvi.

held to affect the reality of their divine authorship. The same conviction extended to the canonical history books, which were regarded as prophetic in character. There seems no doubt that in our Lord's day the entire contents of the Old Testament were received as abidingly valid 'oracles of God',[1] to be treasured, studied, believed and obeyed.

The nature of the authority ascribed to these writings appears from the fact that Israel regarded itself as a theocracy, and its Scriptures as, in effect, the statute-book by which God ruled and judged His people. Those Scriptures contained the laws which He had made for them; they were under obligation to obey His enactments, and flouted them at their peril. For while law-keeping meant prosperity, law-breaking would bring judgment in the form of disaster.[2] The Jews of Christ's day shared this conviction of their forbears. They knew themselves to be the people of God, living under the laws and government of God, and bound to obey His laws under penalty of wrath and judgment. Thus, the religion in which our Lord was brought up was first and foremost a religion of subjection to the authority of a written divine word.

THE TEACHING OF CHRIST[3]

a. His Attitude to the Old Testament

Jesus Christ, so far from rejecting this principle of biblical authority, accepted and built on it, endorsing it with the greatest emphasis and the full weight of His authority. And the authority to which He laid claim was absolute and unqualified. He appealed to no human authority, but put His teaching forward as divine in origin, and therefore eternally valid in its own right. 'My doctrine is not mine, but his that sent me.' 'I have not spoken of myself; but the Father which sent me, he gave me a commandment,

[1] Rom. iii. 2. [2] Lv. xxvi; Dt. xxviii; cf. 2 Ki. xxii. 13

[3] For fuller treatments of Christ's attitude to Scripture, see R. V. G. Tasker, *Our Lord's Use of the Old Testament* (Westminster Chapel, 1953) or Chapter II of *The Old Testament in the New Testament*, 2nd ed. (S.C.M., 1954), and J. W. Wenham, *Our Lord's View of the Old Testament* (Tyndale Press).

what I should say, and what I should speak . . . whatsoever I speak therefore, even as the Father said unto me, so I speak.'[1] Therefore 'heaven and earth shall pass away: but my words shall not pass away'.[2] He told His hearers that their eternal destiny depended on whether, having heard His words, they kept them;[3] for 'he that rejecteth me, and receiveth not my words . . . the word that I have spoken, the same shall judge him in the last day'.[4] He taught 'as one having authority';[5] some were awed, others were shocked, by His authoritative manner. He did not hesitate to challenge and condemn, on His own authority, many accepted Jewish ideas which seemed to Him false. But He never opposed His personal authority to that of the Old Testament. He never qualified the Jewish belief in its absolute authority in the slightest degree. The fact we have to face is that Jesus Christ, the Son of God incarnate, who claimed divine authority for all that He did and taught, both confirmed the absolute authority of the Old Testament for others and submitted to it unreservedly Himself.

There is no lack of evidence for our Lord's attitude to the Old Testament. He prefaces with his regular formula of solemn assertion ('Verily [*amen*] I say unto you') the following emphatic assurance : 'till heaven and earth pass, one jot or one tittle shall in no wise pass from the law'.[6] He quotes Gn. ii. 24—in its context a comment passed by Adam or (more likely) the narrator—as an utterance of God : 'have ye not read, that he which made them at the beginning . . . said . . . ?'[7] He treats arguments from Scripture as having clinching force. When he says 'it is written', that is final. There is no appeal against Scripture, for 'the scripture cannot be broken';[8] God's Word holds good for ever. He constantly upbraids the Jewish theologians for their ignorance and neglect of Scripture; 'Do ye not therefore err, because ye know not the scriptures?'[9] 'Have ye not read . . . ?'[10] 'Go ye and learn what

[1] Jn. vii. 16, xii. 49 f.
[2] Mk. xiii. 31.
[3] Mt. vii. 24 ff.
[4] Jn. xii. 48.
[5] Mk. i. 22; Mt. vii. 29.
[6] Mt. v. 18; cf. Lk. xvi. 17.
[7] Mt. xix. 4 f.
[8] Jn. x. 35.
[9] Mk. xii. 24.
[10] Mt. xii. 3, 5, xix. 4, xxi. 16, 42.

that meaneth . . .'[1] When He comes to disentangle principles of the Mosaic law from the perversions of scribal exegesis,[2] He prefaces a word of warning, lest His purpose be misunderstood. 'Think not that I am come to destroy the law, or the prophets'—you must not suppose that when I contrast what 'was said to them of old time' with what 'I say unto you', I am cancelling Scripture; 'I am not come to destroy, but to fulfil'—to expound Scripture, to exhibit and implement its true meaning, and thus, so far from annulling it, to vindicate and confirm its abiding authority.[3]

As well as endorsing the principle of biblical authority in its application to others, our Lord submitted to it Himself. He read the Old Testament as the word of His Father. His mind was saturated in it, as His teaching showed. He met the tempter by avowing His intention to obey what was written.[4] He kept the law; when His opponents accused Him or His disciples of breaking it, He always replied, not that He or they were exempted from it, but that they were in fact keeping it, and their critics had misunderstood its meaning.[5] His whole

[1] Mt. ix. 13; cf. xii. 7, both quoting Ho. vi. 6.

[2] The case for this view of the scope of Mt. v. 21 ff. is convincingly argued by N. B. Stonehouse, *The Witness of Matthew and Mark to Christ* (Philadelphia, 1944); cf. the general verdict of R. V. G. Tasker, *The Old Testament in the New Testament*, p. 32: 'Our Lord came into conflict with the Pharisees not because He was opposed to the written word of the Law, to which both He and they appealed, but because in His judgment the formalism and the casuistry of the legal system which the Pharisees had superimposed upon the Law rendered them insensitive to the living word of God; . . . What roused His antagonism were such things as the casuistry which justified the practice of Corban; the false deduction that the command to love one's neighbour implied that one should hate one's enemies; the limiting of the divine prohibition of murder and adultery to the specific acts of murder and adultery; the assumption that the only oaths which need be taken seriously were those made by the actual use of the divine name; and the extension of the exception clause in the law of divorce so as to permit divorce "for any cause" whatever.'

[3] Mt. v. 17.

[4] Mt. iv. 1 ff.; Lk. iv. 1 ff.; cf. Mt. xvi. 21–23.

[5] Cf. Mk. ii. 24 ff., iii. 4 f.; Lk. xiii. 14 ff.; Jn. vii. 21 ff.

ministry, as recorded in the Gospels, may justly be described as a prolonged and many-sided affirmation of the authority of the Old Testament. For He drew His conception of the Messianic office entirely from the strands of Old Testament prophecy concerning the One that should come—the Son of David who was the Son of God, the Son of man who should take the kingdom, the Servant who should preach mercy and suffer for the people's sins. He told the congregation at Nazareth that He was preaching in fulfilment of Scripture.[1] Matthew says that He healed in fulfilment of Scripture;[2] indeed, He said as much Himself when, to restore the Baptist's faith in His Messiahship, He appealed to the evidence of His cures in words drawn from the prophetic picture of the day of redemption in Is. xxxv. 5 f.[3] And He went to death in fulfilment of Scripture. As soon as Peter had confessed Him Messiah at Cæsarea Philippi, 'he began to teach them, that the Son of man must suffer many things, and . . . be killed, and after three days rise again'[4]—*must*, because so it was written. 'Behold, we go up to Jerusalem, and all things that are written by the prophets concerning the Son of man shall be accomplished.'[5] 'The Son of man goeth as it is written of him,' He said at the last supper.[6] 'I tell you,' He added a little later, 'that this scripture must be fulfilled in me, "And he was reckoned with transgressors"; for what is written about me has its fulfilment.'[7] When arrested, He checked Peter's impulse to fight for his Master's life: 'Do you think that I cannot appeal to my Father, and he will at once send me more than twelve legions of angels? But how then should the scriptures be fulfilled, that it must be so? . . . All this has taken place, that the scriptures of the prophets might be fulfilled.'[8] He ended a life of obedience to Scripture by dying in obedience to Scripture, looking to His Father to raise Him from

[1] Lk. iv. 18 ff., quoting Is. lxi. 1 ff.
[2] Mt. viii. 16 f., quoting the Greek version of Is. liii. 4.
[3] Mt. xi. 5. [4] Mk. viii. 31; cf. ix. 31, x. 33 f. [5] Lk. xviii. 31.
[6] Mt. xxvi. 24. [7] Lk. xxii. 37, RSV, quoting Is. liii. 12.
[8] Mt. xxvi. 53, 56, RSV.

death in fulfilment of Scripture. Duly he rose; and returned to His disciples to explain to them from Scripture the meaning of what had happened : 'These are my words which I spoke to you, while I was still with you, that everything written about me in the law of Moses and the prophets and the psalms must be fulfilled. . . . Thus it is written, that the Christ should suffer and on the third day rise from the dead, and that repentance and forgiveness of sins should be preached in his name to all nations.'[1]

In life and death, therefore, our Lord devoted Himself to fulfilling the Scriptures. And it was as the fulfiller of Scripture that He presented Himself to the Jews. He claimed to exhibit in Himself what the Old Testament actually meant. He appealed to it as providing the warrant for what He said and did, and the sphere of reference in terms of which alone He could be understood. He saw Himself as the key to it, and it as the key to Himself. Any interpretation of either that was not given in terms of the other would be a misinterpretation. Indeed, He held that anyone who really believed the Old Testament would know who He was, and come to trust Him. 'You search the scriptures,' He told the Jews, 'because you think that in them you have eternal life; and it is they that bear witness to me; yet you refuse to come to me that you may have life. . . . If you believed Moses, you would believe me, for he wrote of me. But if you do not believe his writings, how will you believe my words?'[2] And by His very assertions that the Old Testament bears authoritative divine witness to Him, our Lord bears authoritative divine witness to it.

In short, the Gospels assure us that the historic Israelite belief in the divine authority of the Old Testament was the foundation of Christ's whole ministry. He challenged current interpretations of Scripture, but shared and endorsed the accepted view of its nature and status as an authoritative utterance of God.

[1] Lk. xxiv. 44, 46 f., RSV; cf. verses 25 ff.
[2] Jn. v. 39 f., 46 f., RSV.

b. The Significance of His Teaching

It thus appears that Christ's answer to the problem of authority can be summed up as follows:

1. The Old Testament is to be received on His authority (over and above its own witness to itself) as the authoritative written utterance of God, abidingly true and trustworthy. Its divine authority and His confirm each other, so that not to accept both would be to accept neither.

2. To learn what they must believe and do, His disciples are not to regard His words alone, but to take His teaching and the Old Testament together, reading the old revelation as the presupposition of the new and the new as both expounding and augmenting the old. In conjunction with Christ's teaching, the written word of the Old Testament retains its full, divine authority.

Attempts have been made by some who reject Christ's view of the Old Testament to evade the force of this conclusion. But this can be done only by denying Christ's authority altogether. Christ's claim to be divine is either true or false. If it is true, His Person guarantees the truth of all the rest of His teaching (for a divine Person cannot lie or err); therefore, His view of the Old Testament is true. If His claim is false, there is no compelling reason to believe anything else that He said. If we accept Christ's claims, therefore, we commit ourselves to believe all that He taught—on His authority. If we refuse to believe some part of what He taught, we are in effect denying Him to be the divine Messiah—on our own authority. The question, 'What think ye of the Old Testament?', resolves into the question, 'What think ye of Christ?' And our answer to the first proclaims our answer to the second.

Some, overlooking the organic connection between the two Testaments, have suggested that Christ's deference to the authority of the Old should be understood as deliberate accommodation to the prejudices of His hearers: He appealed to the Old Testament, not because He accepted its authority Himself, but because He knew that they did, and hoped thus to gain a readier acceptance for His own teaching. But the hypothesis is impossible. It clearly assumes that the authority of the Old Testament was no essential part of Christ's teaching, which ideally would stand on its own, independent of the Jewish Scriptures. But as we have just seen, the divine authority of the Old Testament was actually axiomatic for Christ's thought and teaching about His own Person and vocation. He forbade men to view Him as anything other than the Fulfiller of the law and the prophets, for He did not believe Himself to be anything other than that. He was the divine Messiah of whom the Old Testament spoke; He had come into the world to fulfil the Scriptures, and that was what He was doing. He appealed to Scripture as the sole and sufficient warrant for the things that He said and did because it was in conscious obedience to Scripture that He said and did them. If we reject His attitude to the Old Testament, we are saying in effect that He founded Christianity on a fallacy. And if we say He was wrong here, we really imply that He was wrong everywhere; for His view of the nature and authority of the Old Testament underlies all He said and did. If, on the other hand, we believe that His claims and ministry were comprehensively vindicated by His resurrection, we are bound to say that His view of the Old Testament was thereby vindicated also.

The theory of conscious accommodation, then, will not fit the facts. Nor will attempts to evade the significance of our Lord's attitude to the Old Testament by appeal to a 'kenosis' theory of incarnation. On this kind of view, the process of incarnation involved such a resignation of divine knowledge on the Son's part that in matters of this kind He inevitably fell victim to the prejudices and errors of His own age. He became a man of His time, it is said, so that naturally His views about the Old Testament were those of His time; but they need not bind us. This is a common line of thought, but it is clearly inadequate. In the first place, it does not reckon with our Lord's claim that all He taught was divine truth. It is true that He did not profess to know all things. He confessed ignorance, for example, of the time of His return. 'No man, no, not the angels . . . neither the Son' can say when it will be. But the very context of this admission was a claim, made in the previous verse, that all He did affirm possessed the abiding quality of unchanging truth. 'Heaven and earth shall pass away: but my words shall not pass away.'[1] And among His affirmations, as we saw, must be numbered the truth and authority of the Old Testament.

Secondly, this theory, like the other, fails to see the fundamental importance of the Old Testament for our Lord's conception of His calling. It, too, assumes that Christ's ideas about the Old Testament are unessential elements in His thought which can be jettisoned without loss to His real message or to His personal authority. But in fact nothing is more crucial to either. If Christ was mistaken in His view of the Old Testament, He misunderstood His own mission, and was mistaken all along the line. And, as Professor Tasker forcibly remarks, 'If He could be mistaken on matters which He regarded as of the strictest relevance to His own person and ministry, it is difficult to see exactly how or why He can or should be trusted anywhere else.'[2] To undercut Christ's teaching about the authority of the Old Testament is to strike at His own authority at the most fundamental point.

Others tell us that the final authority for Christians is not Scripture, but Christ, whom we must regard as standing apart from Scripture and above it. He is its Judge; and we, as His disciples, must judge Scripture by Him, receiving only what is in harmony with His life and teaching and rejecting all that is not. But who is this Christ, the Judge of Scripture? Not the Christ of the New Testament and of history. That Christ does not judge Scripture; He obeys it and fulfils it. By word and deed He endorses the authority of the whole of it. Certainly, He is the final authority for Christians; that is precisely why Christians are bound to acknowledge the authority of Scripture. Christ teaches them to do so. A Christ who

[1] Mk. xiii. 31, 32. [2] *Op. cit.*, p. 37.

permits His followers to set Him up as the Judge of Scripture, One by whom its authority must be confirmed before it becomes binding and by whose adverse sentence it is in places annulled, is a Christ of human imagination, made in the theologian's own image, One whose attitude to Scripture is the opposite to that of the Christ of history. If the construction of such a Christ is not a breach of the second commandment, it is hard to see what is. It is sometimes said that to treat the Bible as the infallible word of God is idolatry. If Christ was an idolater, and if following His teaching is idolatry, the accusation may stand; not, however, otherwise. But to worship a Christ who did not receive Scripture as God's unerring word, nor require His followers to do so, would seem to be idolatry in the strictest sense.

We conclude, then, that we must reckon seriously with the fact that Christ accepted the principle of biblical authority, on which the life of the Jewish Church was based, and embodied it unchanged in Christianity. Through His coming, new revelation was given, and new books were added to the canon of Scripture, as we shall see; but the principle that the people of God must live in subjection to the written Word of God remained unaltered.

THE TEACHING OF THE APOSTLES

The apostles clearly grasped their Master's teaching about Scripture. They proclaimed Christianity as the fulfilment of Scripture. They preached the authority of Christ on the basis of the authority of the Old Testament. They argued from Scripture, quoting its words as the speech of God.[1] Indeed, they laid claim to the Old Testament as a Christian book. The oracles of God, entrusted to the Jews, had been written primarily, they maintained, for the benefit of Christian believers. 'Whatsoever things were written aforetime were written for our learning.' The events in the wilderness in Moses' day 'were written down for our instruction, upon whom the end of the ages has come'. The prophets who spoke of the sufferings and

[1] Acts iv. 25; Rom. i. 2, ix. 17; Gal. iii. 8, etc.

glory of Christ 'were serving not themselves but you, in the things which have now been announced to you by those who preached the good news to you'.[1] The reckoning of righteousness to believing Abraham was recorded 'not for his sake alone, but for ours also'.[2] The Old Testament Scriptures are 'able to make thee wise unto salvation through faith which is in Christ Jesus'.[3] To Christians, who held the key to its meaning, the Old Testament was luminous, though to those who veiled their hearts by refusing to find its meaning in Christ it remained obscure.[4] This, to the apostles, was precisely the difference between Christians and Jews; not that the latter were still fettered to the authority of the Old Testament while the former were free from its shackles, but that Christians could understand the Old Testament where Jewry could not.

The apostles followed our Lord in recognizing the abiding authority of the Old Testament over the people of God. The Church proclaimed its continuity with Israel, not merely by claiming the Jewish Scriptures as a Christian book, but by treating those Scriptures as God-given law for the guidance of its life. That the true Israel is a community which submits to the authority of the Old Testament was taken for granted; in fact, the Christian case against Jewry was precisely that Christians did this where Jews did not, and that the Jews had un-churched themselves by their refusal to do so. The use of the Old Testament in the New Testament Epistles shows that the churches addressed acknowledged its authority. The Church of the New Testament differed from the Old Testament Church in many ways, as we saw earlier, but in professing subjection to the authority of the Old Testament Scriptures the two were at one.

Not, of course, that the Old Testament contained the only divine teaching that the apostles taught the early Church to acknowledge. Christ's own words were authori-

[1] Rom. xv. 4; 1 Cor. x. 11, RSV; 1 Pet. i. 12, RSV.
[2] Rom. iv. 23 f., RSV.
[3] 2 Tim. iii. 15.
[4] Cf. 2 Cor. iii. 14 ff.

tative;[1] and so were those of the apostles themselves.[2] The apostles claimed an authoritative commission from Christ[3] to act as His representatives in founding and building up the first churches.[4] They presented themselves as Christ's ambassadors,[5] and their message as God's word.[6] They claimed to have received the Holy Ghost in a unique way, so that they might correctly understand the mystery of God's revelation in Christ and proclaim it in normative, authoritative statements, 'not in the words which man's wisdom teacheth, but which the Holy Ghost teacheth'.[7] Their authority had been given them by Christ through His word of commission and His gift of the Spirit. He had promised the twelve that the Spirit should come to teach them what in His own earthly ministry He had left unsaid,[8] and He had kept His promise; so that the apostolic teaching was in reality the complete and final version of His own. Paul is our fullest witness here. He sets up his gospel as a norm of truth.[9] He commands 'in the name (i.e., with the authority) of the Lord Jesus'.[10] One mark of spirituality, he says, is recognition of his authority and submission to it: 'If any one thinks that he is a prophet, or spiritual, he should acknowledge that what I am writing to you is a command of the Lord. If any one does not recognize this, he is not recognized.'[11] The churches must bow to Paul's rulings,[12] and those who will not must be put out of fellowship till they come to a better mind.[13] Apostolic utterances are the truth of Christ and possess the authority of Christ; they are to be received as words of God, because what they convey is, in fact, the word of God.

[1] Cf. Acts xx. 35; 1 Cor. vii. 10 (quoting the words recorded in Mt. v. 32).

[2] For a fuller study of the nature of apostolic authority, see N. Geldenhuys, *Supreme Authority* (Marshall, Morgan & Scott, 1953), pp. 45 ff., and N. B. Stonehouse in *The Infallible Word* (Tyndale Press, 1946), pp. 110 ff.

[3] Gal. i. 1.

[4] Gal. ii. 7 f.; 2 Cor. x. 8, xiii. 10.

[5] 2 Cor. v. 19, 20.

[6] 1 Thes. ii. 13.

[7] 1 Cor. ii. 13.

[8] Jn. xvi. 12 ff.

[9] Gal. i. 8.

[10] 2 Thes. iii. 6; cf. 1 Thes. iv. 2.

[11] 1 Cor. xiv. 37, 38, RSV.

[12] 1 Cor. xi. 2; 2 Thes. ii. 15.

[13] 2 Thes. iii. 6, 14.

THE ATTITUDE OF THE EARLY CHURCH[1]

The early churches received the apostolic teaching (which included the words of Christ) and the Old Testament as two complementary parts of the body of divine revelation which Christ had given them as the rule for their faith and life. It was only natural, therefore, that they should begin to make regular use of apostolic Epistles and apostolically authenticated Gospels, when these appeared, as a basis for teaching and exposition, and as authoritative documents for reading in public worship alongside the Old Testament. The apostles' own requirement that their letters be read to the assembled church had from the first pointed the way to this,[2] and it was, in fact, an obvious step once the nature of the apostles' authority as interpreters of Christ had been recognized. So far as we know, the practice received no discussion; certainly, it needed none.

Not that all apostolic writings were at once put into service as part of the canon of Scripture. Such evidence as there is in the sub-apostolic literature suggests merely that at the end of the first century they were universally held to possess the same divinely authoritative character as the books of the Old Testament.[3] But where this recognition was present, the explicit acknowledgment of them as Scripture was only a matter of time. Indeed, we find Paul's Epistles bracketed with 'the other scriptures' as early as the second Epistle of Peter.[4]

When in the mid-second century the Church began formally to define the limits of its New Testament canon,

[1] The formation of the New Testament canon is a difficult and complex subject which we cannot fully discuss here. There is a helpful treatment in N. B. Stonehouse's chapter on 'The Authority of the New Testament' in *The Infallible Word* (pp. 88 ff.).

[2] Cf. 1 Thes. v. 27; Col. iv. 16; see also Rev. i. 3.

[3] The evidence is reviewed by Geldenhuys, *Supreme Authority*, pp. 90 ff.

[4] 2 Pet. iii. 16. This Epistle is commonly held to be a pseudonymous document dating from the mid-second century: but see our remarks in Appendix II, pp. 182 ff.

it seems that the process involved no more than the explicit recognition of an established state of affairs. It was not a case of imparting to a newly-made collection of books an authority which they had not had before, nor of reminding a forgetful generation what authority the earliest Christians had ascribed to apostolic writings. What evidence there is suggests rather that it was simply a case of settling the limits of a class of books whose authoritative character had never been in doubt; and that it needed doing, not so much because the churches were omitting to use the books they should, as because some were using books that they should not. The criterion used for this task seems to have been a simple historical one; which books are in fact apostolic (i.e., apostolically written or authorized)? The Church reminded itself that the criterion of canonicity is inspiration, and that the ability to teach and write the faith in an inspired form (i.e., a form in which the human words could be regarded as words 'which the Holy Ghost teaches', words from God having normative authority) was an apostolic prerogative; accordingly, it sought to ensure that such regard should not be paid to any book which lacked apostolic authorship or an equivalent apostolic sanction. The evidence we have is too sparse to make it quite clear in what precise sense the writings of such non-apostolic authors as Mark and Luke were regarded as possessing apostolic sanction; what is clear, however, is that they were so regarded, and acknowledged as authoritative on that basis. In fact, the major books in our New Testament—the four Gospels, Paul's Epistles, 1 Peter, 1 John, Acts—were universally recognized from the first; though some of the others had to wait till the fourth century before being accepted by certain sections of the Church. The important thing to grasp as one surveys the intricacies of the history of the canon is that what the Church believed itself to be doing was not creating the New Testament, but recognizing it. God was held to have created it, by inspiring the books destined to compose it; the Church sought merely to discern which books those were.

For the idea of a 'canon' (a set of authoritative Scriptures functioning as a rule of faith and life) was not a second-century invention. It had existed in Christendom from the first, since the Church took over the canonical Jewish Scriptures. And the expectation of a New Testament canon to supplement and complete the Old emerged naturally—indeed inevitably—from the original Christian understanding of Christianity. Christ had bound His Church to live under the authority of the Old Testament, in conjunction with His own teaching and that of the apostles (which was, after all, no more than His own teaching in its completed form). But if the new revelation was to become law for the Church alongside the old, it needed to be put into a permanent written form, as the old had been. And if God had caused His earlier, preliminary revelation to be written, then without doubt He would cause His final, crowning revelation to be recorded in writing. If the New Covenant was the completion and fulfilment of the Old, then it was natural to expect from the God who inspired an authoritative account of the one an authoritative account of the other. When there was an Old Testament, recording the first and more obscure stages in saving revelation, it would have been strange indeed had there been no New Testament, proclaiming God's full and final revelation in Christ, to complete and elucidate it. The inner logic of Christianity thus required an apostolic New Testament as a God-given complement to the Old. The fact that the early Church felt this shows that it understood by what principle of authority it ought to live. We should not hesitate to ascribe the process by which it sought and found a New Testament to the providential guidance of the Holy Ghost, nor to receive that New Testament as from the hand of Christ, as God-breathed Scripture, inspired and, together with the Old Testament, authoritative for faith and life.

THE IMPLICATIONS OF BIBLICAL AUTHORITY

Let us sum up our study. The religion of the New Testament professes to be a perfected form of the religion of the Old Testament; and that religion was based on the principle of biblical authority. Jesus Christ used His personal authority as a divine Teacher to confirm the authority of the Old Testament. The apostles, bearing a unique commission from Christ and being uniquely empowered by His Spirit, claimed Christ's authority for their own teaching; and they treated the authority of the Jewish Scriptures as axiomatic, and imposed them on the infant Church as the Christian Bible. Their own writings claimed, and were credited with, the same divine authority that the Old Testament had. The nature of Christianity, as the completion of Israel's religion, made it virtually certain that God would give the Church an apostolic New Testament, as the completion of Israel's Bible; and this in fact He has done. It is clear that the Christian Church stands in the same relation to its Scriptures as did the Jewish Church to the Old Testament. To deny the normative authority of Scripture over the Church is to misconceive the nature of Christianity, and, in effect, to deny the Lordship of Christ. If the teaching of Christ and the apostles is to rule the Church, the Church must be ruled by Scripture. As the Old Testament was the law by which God governed the Jewish Church, so the Christian Bible—Old and New Testaments together—is the law by which Christ governs His Church today. Christ rules, as Jehovah ruled, by the written Word. Such is the conclusion to which our study of the New Testament doctrine of authority leads. Those who acknowledge the Lordship of Christ are bound to accept the principle of biblical authority.

But let us be clear what this involves. The principle has far-reaching practical implications. It dictates both our approach to Bible study and our use of Scripture in our own and the Church's life. We shall return to the former topic again.[1] Here, we shall only make the general statement that the Bible itself must fix and control the methods and presuppositions with which it is studied. On the latter topic, we would say this : because the Church on earth consists of imperfectly sanctified sinners, there are always two defects in the lives of its members, both corporately and individually. These are ignorance and

[1] See Chapter IV.

error, which cause omissions and mistakes in belief and behaviour. The Church, therefore, has two constant needs; instruction in the truths by which it must live, and correction of the shortcomings by which its life is marred. Scripture is designed to meet this twofold need; it is 'profitable for teaching . . . and for training in righteousness' on the one hand, and for 'reproof' and 'correction' on the other.[1] It is the Church's responsibility to use Scripture for its intended purpose. This it does by the complementary activities of exposition followed by reformation. To accept the authority of Scripture means in practice being willing, first to believe what it teaches, and then to apply its teaching to ourselves for our correction and guidance. The Reformers saw that this was what God demanded of the Church in the sixteenth century; and the truth is that He demands the same in every age of the Church's life. The words and lives of Christian men must be in continual process of reformation by the written Word of their God.

This means that ecclesiastical traditions and private theological speculations may never be identified with the word which God speaks, but are to be classed among the words of men which the Word of God must reform. A moment's thought will show how momentous this conclusion is. Take first the matter of tradition. Whether or not we belong to a communion that treats tradition as an authoritative source of teaching, we are all in fact children of tradition in our religion. We do not start our Christian lives by working out our faith for ourselves; it is mediated to us by Christian tradition, in the form of sermons, books and established patterns of church life and fellowship. We read our Bibles in the light of what we have learned from these sources; we approach Scripture with minds already formed by the mass of accepted opinions and viewpoints with which we have come into contact, in both the Church and the world. Inevitably, we grow up children of our own age, reflecting in our outlook the mental environment in which we were reared. The process is as natural as breathing in the air around us,

[1] 2 Tim. iii. 16, RSV.

and as unconscious. It is easy to be unaware that it has happened; it is hard even to begin to realize how profoundly tradition in this sense has moulded us. But we are forbidden to become enslaved to human tradition, either secular or Christian, whether it be 'catholic' tradition, or 'critical' tradition, or 'ecumenical' tradition, or even 'evangelical' tradition. We may never assume the complete rightness of our own established ways of thought and practice and excuse ourselves the duty of testing and reforming them by Scripture.

Again, whether or not we call ourselves Liberals, we are all in fact inclined to subjectivism in our theology. God's thoughts are not our thoughts, and the God-centred approach which the Bible makes to problems of life and thought is in the highest degree unnatural to the minds of sinful and self-centred men. It calls for a veritable Copernican revolution in our habits of thought, and is slowly and painfully learned. On the other hand, it is entirely natural for sinners to think of themselves as wise, not by reason of divine teaching, but through the independent exercise of their own judgment, and to try to justify their fancied wisdom by adjusting what the Bible teaches to what they have already imbibed from other sources ('modern knowledge'). Professed re-statements of the faith in modern terms often prove to be revisions of the faith to make it square with popular intellectual fashions. This process of assimilating God's revealed truth to the current religious and philosophical opinions of men is the essence of the speculative method in theology which Scripture repudiates. Yet we all constantly do it, more or less; for sin is present with all of us. As usual with sinful habits of mind, we are largely unconscious of our lapses, and only become aware of them as we test ourselves by Scripture and ask God to search our minds and teach us to criticize our own thinking. This, once again, is a discipline that none may shirk.

Scripture, indeed, contains emphatic warnings against uncritical deference to traditions and speculations in theology. Christ deals with the question of the authority of tradition in Mk. vii. 6–13. The Pharisees claimed that their oral law was derived from Moses and should therefore be treated as an authoritative supplement to and exposition of the written law. Christ rejects this idea, contrasting the written word with the oral law as 'the commandment *of God*' and 'the commandments *of men*' respectively. He uses the first to judge the second, and tells the Pharisees that by following the second as against the first they 'lay aside' and 'reject' God's commandment, and 'make the word of God of none effect'. The fact that they are bowing to man-made tradition rather than God-given Scripture, He says, shows that their hearts are far from God. To Christ, ecclesiastical tradition was no part of the word of God; it must be tested by Scripture and, if found wanting, dropped. The New Testament gives no hint that this principle was affected by the transition from the old order to the new.

Nor may speculative revisions of the faith by the light of secular thought be equated with the word of God. Paul affirms this in Col. ii. 8 and 18. Having said, 'as ye . . . received Christ Jesus the Lord, so walk ye in him' (verse 6), he adds this warning: 'see to it that no one makes a prey of you by philosophy . . . according to human tradition . . . and not according to Christ'; 'let no one disqualify you, insisting on self-abasement and worship of angels, taking his stand on visions, puffed up without reason by his sensuous mind, and not holding fast to the Head (Christ)' (RSV). The message preached to the Colossians was 'the word of God', 'the word of the truth of the gospel'; it alone was 'according to Christ', and their salvation depended on holding it fast.[1] But the reconstructed version of it which the religious philosophers of Colossæ had produced (guided, apparently, by a paganized Judaism without and mystical intimations within) was false; inevitably it led away from Christ (as speculative theology always does) and jeopardized men's souls. The principle illustrated here is that no synthesis between the gospel and non-Christian systems is permissible. The gospel is complete in itself; to supplement it with extraneous ideas is not to enrich it, but to pervert it; to

[1] Col. i. 25, 5, 23.

amalgamate it with pagan religions and philosophies is, indeed, to destroy it. The apostolic gospel, which is the word of God, says Paul, must judge all such speculative syntheses. This principle still holds good, although we now have the apostolic word in written not in oral form.

We conclude, then, that the Church must seek, first, to expound Scripture and, second, to reform its belief and practice, where these have erred, by the biblical teaching. This is the theological method which Christ commands His Church to follow: to use Scripture as the rule of faith and life. And the practical proof that Christians accept the authority of Scripture is that they do, in fact, use it in this way.

THE PRESENT ISSUE

Now at last we are in a position to appreciate the fundamental cleavage between so-called 'Fundamentalists' and their critics. The latter are, in fact, subjectivists in the matter of authority. Their position is based on an acceptance of the presuppositions and conclusions of nineteenth-century critical Bible study, which are radically at variance with the Bible's own claims for itself. On this basis, they think it necessary to say—indeed, to insist—that some scriptural assertions are erroneous. Therefore, they cannot accept the axiom that whatever Scripture is found to assert is part of the word of God; for untruths cannot be God's word. Hence they think it impossible to take seriously the 'Jewish' conception of the nature of God-given Scripture which Christ and the Bible teach. Instead, they say, we must use our Christian wits to discern beneath the fallible words of fallible men the eternal truth of God. But this makes it impossible to regard Scripture as authoritative without qualification; what is now authoritative is not Scripture as it stands, but Scripture as pruned by a certain type of scholarship—in other words, human opinions about Scripture. It is true that these critics pay lip-service to the principle of biblical authority, and, indeed, suppose themselves to accept it; but their view of the nature of Scripture effectively prevents them from doing so. It is evident that they have not thought out with sufficient seriousness what subjection to biblical authority means in practice. Their view really amounts to saying that the question of authority is now closed; the supreme authority is undoubtedly Christian reason, which must hunt for the word of God in the Bible by the light of rationalistic critical principles; and a frank recognition of this should henceforth be the starting-point for all our theological thinking. This is all too plainly what they mean when they tell us (as they often do) that biblical criticism has come to stay.

Consequently, we find that the only problem about the Bible which they recognize as outstanding is to formulate a doctrine of the word of God in Scripture which allows for the presence of error there too, and to lay down principles of interpretation for extracting the wheat from the chaff. Therefore, it does not occur to them to treat the evangelical approach to Scripture as anything more than one point of view on this problem; and so they see no more in it than a clumsy style of exegesis springing from a cramping assumption of factual inerrancy. This is illustrated by Dr. Hebert's *Fundamentalism and the Church of God*, which criticizes the evangelical approach to Scripture on the grounds of a proneness to overlook the literary character of imaginative passages, to draw unwarrantable inferences from texts, and to ascribe scientific status to non-scientific statements. Whether or not this is fair comment (and we do not deny that Evangelicals have on occasion laid themselves open to such charges), it misses altogether the central evangelical contention about Scripture, which Hebert does not see at all: namely, that Scripture has complete and final authority over the Church as a self-contained, self-interpreting revelation from God.[1] But this is what Evangelicals are concerned above all to maintain. What Scripture says, God says; and what God says in Scripture is to be the rule of faith and life in His Church.

[1] In the three pages which he allots to the discussion of authority (pp. 24 ff.), Dr. Hebert simply makes a general affirmation of the authority of Christ and of the gospel, and does not mention Christ's teaching on biblical authority at all.

The crucial issue which underlies the 'Fundamentalism' controversy thus concerns the attitude in which Christians should approach Scripture, and the use which they should make of it. Evangelicals seek to approach and use it as it demands that men should; that is, they seek to think and live in accordance with its authoritative teaching. Accordingly, they hold that view of the nature and interpretation of Scripture which they believe to be the Bible's own; and they reject views which they believe to be contrary to it. They reject, for instance, the supposition that Scripture errs; for Scripture claims not to err. They reject all methods of biblical criticism which assume about Scripture something other than Scripture assumes about itself. They reject all approaches to Scripture which would not permit it to function in the Church as a final authority. They will not become subjectivists to order. They regard as mistaken those who believe themselves to acknowledge the authority of the Bible while adopting principles of biblical criticism which Scripture repudiates. They reject as misguided all attempts to weld different theological traditions together without seeking to reform them by the Bible. And they do not believe that agreement is possible in this present controversy till both sides have shown the reality of their acceptance of the Lordship of Christ by adopting the biblical interpretation of the principle of biblical authority, and the method of theological procedure which the Bible itself requires.

CHAPTER IV

SCRIPTURE

I want to know one thing, the way to heaven. . . . God himself has condescended to teach the way. . . . He hath written it down in a book. O give me that book: At any price give me the book of God! I have it: here is knowledge enough for me. Let me be Homo unius libri*. . . . I sit down alone: only God is here. In His presence I open, I read His book; for this end, to find the way to heaven. . . . Does any thing appear dark and intricate? I lift up my heart to the Father of Lights. . . . I then search after and consider parallel passages. . . . I meditate thereon. . . . If any doubt still remain, I consult those who are experienced in the things of God: and then the writings whereby, being dead, they yet speak. And what I thus learn, that I teach.*

JOHN WESLEY

And now, O Lord God, thou art God, and thy words are true.

2 SAMUEL vii. 28, RSV

THE evangelical view of the Bible has come under fire in this controversy, and it is desirable, as the next step in our argument, to re-state it. We have just established the principle that Scripture, 'God's Word written', is the final authority for all matters of Christian faith and practice; and we must follow the method which this principle dictates. Accordingly, we shall ask Scripture to give account of itself, and test human ideas about it by its own teaching. 'Scripture' is a biblical concept; and it is the biblical doctrine of Scripture which Evangelicals are concerned to believe. We shall now try to see what that doctrine is; and our study will show us, incidentally, what reply Evangelicals should make to those who upbraid them for holding theories of dictation, or inerrancy, or literalism.

We must first be clear as to the nature of our task. Our aim is to formulate a biblical doctrine; we are to appeal to Scripture for information about itself, just as we should appeal to it for information on any other doctrinal topic. That means that our formulation will certainly not give a final or exhaustive account of its subject. All doctrines terminate in mystery; for they deal with the works of God, which man in this world cannot fully comprehend, nor has God been pleased fully to explain. 'We know in part'[1] —and only in part. Consequently, however successful our attempt to state the biblical doctrine of Scripture may be, it will not put us in a position where we 'have all the answers', any more than a right statement of the doctrine of the Trinity, or providence, would do. We do not, in fact, expect to give all the answers, and a mere complaint that we leave some problems unsolved will not, of itself, be valid criticism of what we say, any more than it ever would be of any theological exposition; for incompleteness is of the essence of theological knowledge. This, of course, is to a greater or less degree the case with all our knowledge of facts. We never know everything about anything. But clearly, when we creatures come to study the Creator and His ways, we must expect our knowledge to be more fragmentary and partial, and further from being exhaustive, than when we study created things. We make no apology, therefore, for leaving some questions unanswered. All that we are trying to do here is simply to find and demarcate the Bible's own attitude and approach to itself, and to present the relevant biblical material from a properly biblical perspective, so that the scriptural way of regarding and employing Scripture may become clear. The sole test of the adequacy of our account will be this : are we putting matters as the Bible itself puts them? Scripture itself is alone competent to judge our doctrine of Scripture.

The relevant evidence for our purpose is the New Testament doctrine of the Old. Since the two Testaments are of a piece, what is true of one will be true of both. The biblical concept of 'Scripture' will cover all that falls into the category of Scripture.

Space does not permit a full-length treatment, but we shall try to sketch out at least the main points in the Bible's view of the following three topics : its divine origin; its nature as the word of God; and its interpretation.

[1] 1 Cor. xiii. 9.

I. THE DIVINE ORIGIN OF SCRIPTURE[1]

It is customary to use the term *inspiration* to refer to the divine origin of Scripture. The biblical warrant for this is the phrase 'given by inspiration of God' which is used in the Authorized Version to render the adjective *theopneustos* in 2 Tim. iii. 16. As B. B. Warfield showed, this Greek word actually means 'breathed out by God'—not so much *in*-spired as *ex*-spired; so that the text explicitly teaches the divine origin of 'all Scripture'—here, the written word of the Old Testament.[2] As we have seen already, the divine origin of the Old Testament is everywhere assumed in the New Testament.

When we use the phrase 'inspiration of Scripture', the noun may be taken either passively, as meaning 'inspiredness', or actively, as denoting the divine activity by which God-breathed Scripture was produced. In this sense, inspiration is to be defined as a supernatural, providential influence of God's Holy Spirit upon the human authors which caused them to write what He wished to be written for the communication of revealed truth to others. It was a divine activity which, whether or not it had any unusual psychological effects (sometimes it did, sometimes it did not), effectively secured the written transmission of saving truth; in this respect, it is something quite distinct from the 'inspiration' of the creative artist, which secures no such result, and it is more confusing than helpful to try to relate the two things together. It is true that some of those who were 'inspired' in the theological sense were also 'inspired' literary artists in the secular sense—Isaiah or John, for instance; but this comparison obscures the point of the idea of inspiration put forward in 2 Tim. iii. 16, which is simply of a divine activity that produced

[1] For a thorough examination of the biblical material, see B. B. Warfield, *The Inspiration and Authority of the Bible* (Marshall, Morgan and Scott, 1951), especially his definitive study of 'The Biblical Idea of Inspiration' (Chapter III). This study and its companion, 'The Biblical Idea of Revelation', also appear as Chapters I and II in *Biblical Foundations*, a symposium of Warfield's writings (Tyndale Press, 1958, 15*s*.).

[2] *The Inspiration and Authority of the Bible*, pp. 245 ff.

Scripture—one, in other words, which involved human writers as a means to an end, but which actually terminated, not on them, but on what they wrote.

Inspiration did not necessarily involve an abnormal state of mind on the writer's part, such as a trance, or vision, or hearing a voice. Nor did it involve any obliterating or overriding of his personality. Scripture indicates that God in His providence was from the first preparing the human vehicles of inspiration for their predestined task,[1] and that He caused them in many cases, perhaps in most, to perform that task through the normal exercise of the abilities which He had given them. We may not suppose that they always knew they were writing canonical Scripture, even when they consciously wrote with divine authority; and it is not obvious that the writers of, for example, the Song of Solomon, Agur's testament (Pr. xxx), Heman's black Psalm (Ps. lxxxviii), or Luke's Gospel (written, the author tells us, because 'it seemed good to me'), were aware of any directly supernatural prompting at all. Scripture also shows us that inspired documents may be the product of first-hand historical research (as Luke's gospel is[2]), and of direct dependence on older written sources (as Chronicles depends on Kings), and even of wholesale borrowing (compare 2 Peter and Jude). Moreover, it appears that biblical books may have passed through several editions and recensions over the centuries before reaching their final form, as the book of Proverbs certainly did.[3]

a. Dictation?

Because Evengelicals hold that the biblical writers were completely controlled by the Holy Spirit, it is often supposed, as we saw, that they maintain what is called the 'dictation' or 'typewriter' theory of inspiration—namely, that the mental activity of the writers was simply suspended, apart from what was necessary for the mechanical transcription of words supernaturally introduced

[1] Cf. Je. i. 5; Is. xlix. 1, 5; Gal. i. 15. [2] Lk. i. 3.
[3] Cf. Pr. x. i, xxiv. 23, xxv. 1.

into their consciousness.[1] But it is not so. This 'dictation theory' is a man of straw. It is safe to say that no Protestant theologian, from the Reformation till now, has ever held it; and certainly modern Evangelicals do not hold it. We are glad that Dr. Hebert, at least, recognizes this.[2] It is true that many sixteenth- and seventeenth-century theologians spoke of Scripture as 'dictated by the Holy Ghost'; but all they meant was that the authors wrote word for word what God intended. The language of dictation was invoked to signify not the method or psychology of God's guidance of them, but simply the fact and result of it; not the nature of their own mental processes, but the relation of what they wrote to the divine intention. The use of the term 'dictation' was always figurative, and the whole point of the figure lay in the fact that it asserted this relation. It was never used with psychological overtones. The proof of this lies in the fact that, when these theologians addressed themselves to the question, What was the Spirit's mode of operating in the writers' minds?, they all gave their answer in terms not of dictation, but of *accommodation*, and rightly maintained that God completely adapted His inspiring activity to the cast of mind, outlook, temperament, interests, literary habits and stylistic idiosyncrasies of each writer.

b. Accommodation

Those who credit Evangelicals with belief in 'dictation' often appeal to the thought of accommodation as the correct alternative to that view, but in so doing they misunderstand the biblical idea of accommodation no less seriously than they misunderstand the biblical idea of complete divine control. They speak as if it were self-evident that a revelation of truth transmitted through the instrumentality of sinful men would suffer in the process. We are told that, since the biblical writers were imperfect creatures, morally, spiritually and intellectually limited, children of their age and children of Adam too, it was inevitable that crudities, distortions and errors should creep into what they wrote. It is claimed that this is a

[1] See p. 10 above; and Appendix I, pp. 178 f. [2] *Op. cit.*, p. 56.

liberating notion which throws a flood of light on the real character of Scripture, and makes possible a great advance in theological understanding. But does it? It certainly gives the theologian an easy way out when he meets passages that do not square with his idea of what the Bible tells us, or ought to tell us; but is the practice of dismissing awkward details as human corruptions of the pure word of God a biblical way of treating Scripture? It is irrelevant and mischievous to appeal in this connection, as some do, to the example of Christ and the apostles in setting aside Old Testament regulations; for they did this because they recognized that the time had ended for which those regulations were meant to be binding, not because they doubted their divine origin.

In fact, this 'liberating notion' is a mistaken idea which reflects a thoroughly defective approach to the written Word. For, in the first place, it flatly contradicts the New Testament witness that every part of Scripture has a divine origin and all that is written (*pasa graphe*) is *theopneustos*.[1] And, in the second place, it plainly implies that God was somehow constrained, hampered and indeed frustrated in His revelatory purpose by the quality of the human material through which He worked. But this is to deny the biblical doctrine of providence, according to which God 'worketh all things after the counsel of his own will'.[2] The Bible excludes the idea of a frustrated Deity. 'Whatsoever the Lord pleased, that did he in heaven, and in earth.'[3] He was well able to prepare, equip and overrule sinful human writers so that they wrote nothing but what He intended; and Scripture tells us that this is what in fact He did. We are to think of the Spirit's inspiring activity, and, for that matter, of all His regular operations in and upon human personality, as (to use an old but valuable technical term) *concursive*; that is, as exercised in, through and by means of the writers' own activity, in such a way that their thinking and writing was *both* free and spontaneous on their part *and* divinely elicited and controlled, and what they wrote was not only their own work but also God's work. Thus, quotations

[1] Mt. v. 18; 2 Tim. iii. 16. [2] Eph. i. 11. [3] Ps. cxxxv. 6.

from the Psalms in Acts are described both as David's words, the issue of his own God-given knowledge and God-guided reasoning, and as God's words spoken through David's mouth.[1] David was a sinful man; but his words in these cases were the words of God.

c. Providence

The twin suppositions which liberal critics make—that, on the one hand, divine control of the writers would exclude the free exercise of their natural powers, while, on the other hand, divine accommodation to the free exercise of their natural powers would exclude complete control of what they wrote—are really two forms of the same mistake. They are two ways of denying that the Bible can be both a fully human and fully divine composition. And this denial rests (as all errors in theology ultimately do) on a false doctrine of God; here particularly, of His providence. For it assumes that God and man stand in such a relation to each other that they cannot both be free agents in the same action. If man acts freely (i.e., voluntarily and spontaneously), God does not, and *vice versa*. The two freedoms are mutually exclusive. But the affinities of this idea are with Deism, not Christian Theism. It is Deism which depicts God as the passive onlooker rather than the active governor of His world, and which assures us that the guarantee of human freedom lies in the fact that men's actions are not under God's control. But the Bible teaches rather that the freedom of God, who works in and through His creatures, leading them to act according to their nature, is itself the foundation and guarantee of the freedom of their action. It is therefore a great mistake to think that the freedom of the biblical writers can be vindicated only by denying full divine control over them; and the prevalence of this mistake should be ascribed to the insidious substitution of deistic for theistic ideas about God's relation to the world which has been, perhaps, the most damaging effect of modern science on theology. When the critics of Evangelicalism take it for granted that Evangelicals, since they believe in complete control, must hold

[1] Acts i. 16, iv. 25.

the 'dictation' theory, while they themselves, since they recognize accommodation, are bound to hold that in Scripture false and misleading words of men are mixed up with the pure word of God, they merely show how unbiblical their idea of providence has become. The cure for such fallacious reasoning is to grasp the biblical idea of God's *concursive operation* in, with and through the free working of man's own mind.

d. The Analogy of the Person of Christ

A further way in which some critics try to make the point that they do justice to the human character of the Bible, while Evangelicals do not, is by comparing their own position to the orthodox doctrine of the two natures of Christ, and the evangelical view, as they understand it, to the Monophysite heresy. So Dr. Hebert writes: 'The Liberals of the last generation, like critical scholars today, were asserting the vital theological truth of the human nature of the Bible, which is analogous to that of the human nature of Christ. They were in fact fighting against the Monophysite heresy which, with its denial of the true humanity of our Lord, is the favourite heresy of orthodox Christians—who are inclined so to exalt Him as their divine Saviour that they lose sight of the fact that He was and is also truly man.'[1] The suggestion is that Evangelicals fall into an analogous heresy with regard to Scripture. Dr. Hebert goes on to quote some words of Professor R. H. Fuller to this effect, which conclude thus: 'All the way through, we have to discern the treasure in the earthen vessels: the divinity in Christ's humanity . . . the Word of God in the fallible words of men.' Hebert regards this line of criticism as 'very important';[2] but, in fact, he and Professor Fuller misconceive the bearing of the Christological parallel. In so far as it is valid, it confirms the evangelical view of Scripture as against theirs, as we shall now see. We would make the following observations upon it:

1. At best, the analogy between the divine-human person of the Word made flesh, who is Christ, and the divine-

[1] *Op. cit.*, pp. 76 f. [2] *Op. cit.*, p. 78.

human product of the Word written, which is Scripture, can be only a limited one.

2. If the point of the analogy is merely that human as well as divine qualities are to be recognized in Scripture, we can only agree, and add that it should be clear from what we have already said—which is no more than Evangelicals have said constantly for over a century—that we do in fact recognize the reality of both.

3. If we are to carry the analogy further, and take it as indicating something about the character which the human element has by virtue of its conjunction with the divine, we must say that it points directly to the fact that, as our Lord, though truly man, was truly free from sin, so Scripture, though a truly human product, is truly free from error.[1] If the critics believe that Scripture, as a human book, errs, they ought, by the force of their own analogy, to believe also that Christ, as man, sinned.

4. If we are to carry the analogy further still, and take it as indicating something about the reality of the union between the divine and the human, we must say that it is in fact the approach of Evangelicals to Scripture which corresponds to Christological orthodoxy, while that of their critics really corresponds to the Nestorian heresy. Nestorianism begins by postulating a distinction between Jesus as a man and the divine Son, whom it regards as someone distinct, indwelling the man; but then it cannot conceive of the real personal identity of the man and the Son. The right and scriptural way in Christology is to start by recognizing the unity of our Lord's Person as divine and to view His humanity only as an aspect of His

[1] Warfield works this out in detail: 'as, in the case of Our Lord's person, the human nature remains truly human while yet it can never fall into sin or error because it can never act out of relation with the Divine nature into conjunction with which it has been brought; so in the case of the production of Scripture by the conjoint action of human and Divine factors, the human factors have acted as human factors, and have left their mark on the product as such, and yet cannot have fallen into that error which we say it is human to fall into, because they have not acted apart from the Divine factors, by themselves, but only under their unerring guidance'. *The Inspiration and Authority of the Bible*, pp. 162 f.; *Biblical Foundations*, pp. 74 f.

Person, existing within it and never, therefore, dissociated from it. Similarly, the right way to think of Scripture is to start from the biblical idea that the written Scriptures as such are 'the oracles of God' and to study their character as a human book only as one aspect of their character as a divine book. Those who start by postulating a distinction between the Bible as a human book and the word of God that is in it are unable, on their own premises, to recognize and exhibit the real oneness of these two things, and when they try to state their mutual relationship they lapse into an arbitrary subjectivism. This is what happens to the critics. (Incidentally, once we see this, we see why they are so ready to accuse Evangelicals of Monophysitism; for Nestorians have always regarded orthodox Christology as Monophysite.) We must dissent, therefore, from Professor Fuller's Nestorian assertion that our task is to discern the divinity in Christ's humanity and the word of God in the fallible words of man, and suggest that it is rather to appreciate the true manhood of the divine Word incarnate and the authentic human character of the inerrant divine Word written.

II. THE NATURE OF SCRIPTURE

a. The Unity of Scripture

We come now to discuss the nature of the Bible, considered as a single entity—the organism of Scripture, as we may call it. Our first point here is that Scripture is a real *unity*.

The literary historian sees the Bible as a library : a miscellaneous set of more or less occasional writings—public records, legal and liturgical documents, history books, lyric and philosophical poetry and visionary prose, hymns, letters, sermons—put together over a period of a thousand years or more. But it is more than a library of books by human authors; it is a single book with a single author—God the Spirit—and a single theme—God the Son, and the Father's saving purposes, which all revolve round Him. Our Lord is therefore the key to Scripture, and its focal centre; there is a sense in which all bears witness of

Him,[1] and in this common reference the heterogeneous contents of the Bible find their unity. Not that all parts of Scripture are equally important, or witness to Christ and the kingdom of God in the same way. But no part of Scripture is without its bearing on these central topics, and no part of Scripture is rightly understood if read without this reference.[2] The course of redemptive history included apostasies, judgments and captivities, yet that history formed a God-guided unity, and these apparently unproductive episodes served to advance its course towards its predestined goal. And, in the same way, Scripture contains passages which seem unedifying in isolation, yet all these, when set in the context of the whole, contribute something of their own to the biblical message. The structural interrelation of the various parts of the organism of Scripture is certainly complex, but it yields progressively to patient study.

b. The Word of God

It is customary to speak of the Bible, thus regarded, as *the Word of God*. This phrase is applied in the Old Testament both to individual revelations to and utterances by the prophets (every such communication being 'the word of God' or 'of the Lord'), and also to the totality of God's verbal revelation to Israel, as such;[3] and in the New Testament, as we saw, it is used to refer comprehensively to the body of revealed truths which made up the apostolic gospel.[4] The phrase declares the divine origin of that to which it applies: whatever is denominated 'the word of God' is thereby affirmed to be a divine utterance. It is for this reason that the phrase is applied to the Bible. The purpose of this usage is to make explicit the biblical conception of Scripture—which is that Scripture is the sum total of divine revelation recorded in a God-breathed written form, and that every scriptural statement is there-

[1] Jn. v. 39; Lk. xxiv. 27, 44 ff. [2] Cf. 2 Cor. iii. 14–16.

[3] See Ps. cxix, where God's 'word' (singular: *dabhar* or *imra*, 42 times) is a synonym for His 'law' (*torah*, instruction), 'testimonies', 'precepts', 'statutes', 'commandments', etc.

[4] See p. 42 above.

fore to be received as a divine utterance. The New Testament writers regarded Scripture as the written Word of God, made up of the written words of God—as, in fact, 'the oracles of God'.[1] No clearer proof of this could be given than Warfield's survey of 'two classes of passages, each of which, when taken separately, throws into the clearest light their (the New Testament writers') habitual appeal to the Old Testament text as to God Himself speaking, while, together, they make an irresistible impression of the absolute identification by their writers of the Scriptures in their hands with the living voice of God. In one of these classes of passages the Scriptures are spoken of as if they were God; in the other, God is spoken of as if He were the Scriptures : in the two together, God and the Scriptures are brought into such conjunction as to show that in point of directness of authority no distinction was made between them.

'Examples of the first class of passages are such as these : Gal. iii. 8, "The Scripture, foreseeing that God would justify the heathen through faith, preached before the gospel unto Abraham, saying, In thee shall all the nations be blessed" (Gen. xii 1–3); Rom. ix. 17. "The Scripture saith unto Pharaoh, Even for this same purpose have I raised thee up" (Ex. ix. 16). It was not, however, the Scripture (which did not exist at the time) that, foreseeing God's purposes of grace in the future, spoke these precious words to Abraham, but God Himself in His own person : it was not the not-yet-existent Scripture that made this announcement to Pharaoh, but God Himself through the mouth of His prophet Moses. These acts could be attributed to "Scripture" only as the result of such habitual identification, in the mind of the writer, of the text of Scripture with God as speaking, that it became natural to use the term "Scripture says" when what was really intended was "God, as recorded in Scripture, said".

'Examples of the other class of passages are such as these : Matt. xix. 4, 5, "And he answered and said, Have ye not read that he which made them from the beginning

[1] Rom. iii. 2; see Warfield, *The Inspiration and Authority of the Bible*, Chapter VIII, for a thorough discussion of this phrase.

made them male and female, and said, For this cause shall a man leave his father and mother, and shall cleave to his wife, and the twain shall become one flesh?" (Gen. ii. 24); Heb. iii. 7, "Wherefore, even as the Holy Ghost saith, Today if ye shall hear his voice", etc. (Ps. xcv. 7); Acts iv. 24, 25, "Thou art God, who by the mouth of thy servant David hast said, Why do the heathen rage and the people imagine vain things" (Ps. ii. 1); Acts xiii. 34, 35, "He that raised him up from the dead, now no more to return to corruption . . . hath spoken in this wise, I will give you the holy and sure blessings of David" (Isa. lv. 3); "because he saith also in another [Psalm], Thou wilt not give thy holy one to see corruption" (Ps. xvi. 10); Heb. i. 6, "And when he again bringeth in the first born into the world, he saith, And let all the angels of God worship him" (Deut. xxxii. 43); "and of the angels he saith, Who maketh his angels wings, and his ministers a flame of fire" (Ps. civ. 4); "but of the Son, *he saith,* Thy Throne, O God, is for ever and ever", etc. (Ps. xlv. 7); and, "Thou, Lord, in the beginning", etc. (Ps. cii. 36). It is not God, however, in whose mouth these sayings are placed in the text of the Old Testament: they are the words of others, recorded in the text of Scripture as spoken to or of God. They could be attributed to God only through such habitual identification, in the minds of the writers, of the text of Scripture with the utterances of God that it had become natural to use the term "God says" when what was really intended was "Scripture, the Word of God, says".

'The two sets of passages, together, thus show an absolute identification, in the minds of these writers, of "Scripture" with the speaking God.'[1]

Now the divine utterances of which Old Testament Scripture was composed were held, as we saw, to coalesce into the unity of a single message. The very use of the terms 'Scripture' (*graphé*) and 'the Scriptures' (*hai graphai*) in the New Testament proves this. At the conclusion of a careful survey of this usage, Warfield records the following just verdict: 'The employment of *graphe*

[1] Warfield, *op. cit.*, pp. 299 ff.

in the NT so far follows its profane usage, in which it is prevailingly applied to entire documents and carries with it a general implication of completeness, that in its more common reference it designates the OT to which it is applied in its completeness as a unitary whole. . . . It remains only to add that the same implication is present in the designation of the OT as *hai graphai*, which, . . . does not suggest that the OT is a collection of "treatises", but is merely a variant of *he graphe* in accordance with good Greek usage, employed interchangeably with it at the dictation of nothing more recondite than literary habit. Whether *hai graphai* is used, then, or *he graphe*, or the anarthrous *graphe*, in each case alike the OT is thought of as a single document set over against all other documents by reason of its unique Divinity and indefectible authority, by which it is constituted in every passage and declaration the final arbiter of belief and practice."[1]

The biblical concept of Scripture, then, is of a single, though complex, God-given message, set down in writing in God-given words; a message which God has spoken and still speaks. On the analogy of scriptural usage, therefore, it is evident that to describe Scripture as the Word of God written is entirely accurate. Accordingly, if when we speak of 'the Bible' we mean not just a quantity of printed paper, but a written document declaring a message—if, that is, we view the inspired volume as a literary product, a verbal expression of thought—then 'the Bible' and 'Scripture' will be synonyms : it will thus be correct to call the Bible the Word of God, and to affirm that what it says, God says. If, on the other hand, we are thinking of the Bible simply as a printed book, it will not be wrong to say that the Bible *contains* the Word of God, in the same sense in which any other book *contains* the pronouncements of its author. To speak in these terms, however, is to invite misunderstanding, since Liberal theologians have been in the habit of using this formula to insinuate that part of what the Bible contains is no part

[1] *Dictionary of Christ and the Gospels*, ed. Hastings, s.v. 'Scripture' II. 586; reprinted in Warfield, *op. cit.*, pp. 238 f.

of the Word of God. It is worth guarding our language in order to avoid seeming to endorse so unbiblical a view.

The scriptural approach to Scripture is thus to regard it as God's written testimony to Himself. When we call the Bible the Word of God, we mean, or should mean, that its message constitutes a single utterance of which God is the author. What Scripture says, He says. When we hear or read Scripture, that which impinges on our mind (whether we realize it or not) is the speech of God Himself.

Not that the Church knows, or ever knew, or will know in this world, the full meaning of God's Word. As we shall point out more fully later, the task of biblical interpretation never ends. There is no such thing as an exhaustive exegesis of any passage. The Holy Spirit is constantly showing Christian men facets of revealed truth not seen before. To claim finality for any historic mode of interpretation or system of theology would be to resist the Holy Ghost; there is always more to be said, and the Church of each age should echo John Robinson's confidence that the Lord has more light and truth yet to break out of His holy Word. Our point here is simply that the Church must receive all teaching that proves to be biblical, whether on matters of historical or of theological fact, as truly part of God's Word.[1]

This shows the importance of insisting that the inspiration of Scripture is *verbal*. Words signify and safeguard meaning; the wrong word distorts the intended sense. Since God inspired the biblical text in order to communicate His Word, it was necessary for him to ensure that the words written were such as did in fact convey it. We do not stress the verbal character of inspiration from a super-

[1] It has been pointed out to me that the use of the phrase 'word of God' in this book may cause confusion if it is not explained. The rule is that when 'word' is spelt with a capital 'W', the reference is to Scripture, or the total biblical message. When it is spelt with a small 'w', the reference is to some particular divine utterance, such as the Christian gospel (which is what the phrase denotes in the New Testament, as we saw). Every such word of God is itself part of the Word of God, which is the normative account of all that God says to His Church.

stitious regard for the original Hebrew and Greek words (like that of Islam for its Koran, which is held to consist essentially of Arabic words, and therefore to be untranslatable); we do so from a reverent concern for the sense of Scripture. If the words were not wholly God's, then their teaching would not be wholly God's.

This consideration suggests a further problem, at which we may here glance: how is it warrantable to treat the Bible as we actually have it as the Word of God, when we have no reason to think that any manuscript or version now existing is free from corruptions? It is sometimes suggested that the evangelical view of Scripture can have no practical application or significance, since the faultless autographs which it posits are not available to us, and that in practice we are involved in an inescapable subjectivism by the necessity of relying on conjectural reconstructions of the text. The suggestion here is that we can have no confidence that any text that we possess conveys to us the genuine meaning of the inspired Word. It is, of course, true that textual corruptions are no part of the authentic Scriptures, and that no text is free from such slips. But faith in the consistency of God warrants an attitude of confidence that the text is sufficiently trustworthy not to lead us astray. If God gave the Scriptures for a practical purpose—to make men wise unto salvation through faith in Christ—it is a safe inference that He never permits them to become so corrupted that they can no longer fulfil it. It is noteworthy that the New Testament men did not hesitate to trust the words of the Old Testament as they had it as reliable indications of the mind of God. This attitude of faith in the adequacy of the text is confirmed, so far as it can be, by the unanimous verdict of textual scholars that the biblical text is excellently preserved, and no point of doctrine depends on any of the small number of cases in which the true reading remains doubtful. Professor F. F. Bruce expresses the verdict of scholarship as well as of biblical faith when he writes: 'By the "singular care and providence" of God the Bible text has come down to us in such substantial purity that even the most uncritical edition of the Hebrew or Greek

. . . cannot effectively obscure the real message of the Bible, or neutralize its saving power."[1]

This is not to say that textual criticism is needless and unprofitable; but it is to say that, while the work of recovering the original text is not yet finished, and no doubt never will be finished in every minute particular, we should not hesitate to believe that the text as we have it is substantially correct, and may safely be trusted as conveying to us the Word of God with sufficient accuracy for all practical purposes. God's faithfulness to His own intentions is our guarantee of that.

c. *Propositional Revelation*

The Word of God consists of *revealed truths*. This is nowadays an unfashionable notion. It is commonly said that there are no revealed truths; God revealed Himself, not by words, but by the mighty redemptive works through which He became the world's Saviour. Revelation is by action, not by instruction. The Bible is not revelation, but a memorial and legacy of revelation : a record of observations, impressions and opinions of godly men involved in redemptive history. It has the relative authority of a first-hand account, written with thought and care by men of good faith and great insight, but it has not the absolute authority of truth. Later generations must use their own insight to decide how far its reports may be taken as true, or its theology as adequate. No finality attaches to what it says; it is a source and quarry for theology, but not a standard or criterion for it. It is the work of pious men using their God-given abilities to interpret and explain the acts of God—in other words, a piece of godly speculation; and it forms the jumping-off ground for the religious enquiry and reflection of later ages—which is also, of course, no more than godly speculation. Scriptural statements are simply human testimonies to revela-

[1] 'As Originally Given' (a comment on the reference in the I.V.F. doctrinal basis to 'the divine inspiration and infallibility of Holy Scripture, as originally given'), in *The Theological Students' Fellowship Terminal Letter*, Spring 1956, p. 3. The phrase in inverted commas is from the Westminster Confession, I. viii.

tion, fallible and inadequate as all man's words are. They must not be equated with a verbal word of God; there is, in fact, no such word.

But according to Scripture, God reveals Himself to men both by exercising power for them and by teaching truth to them. The two activities are not antithetical, but complementary. Indeed, the biblical position is that the mighty acts of God are not revelation to man at all, except in so far as they are accompanied by words of God to explain them. Leave man to guess God's mind and purpose, and he will guess wrong; he can know it only by being told it. Moreover, the whole purpose of God's mighty acts is to bring man to know Him by faith; and Scripture knows no foundation for faith but the spoken word of God, inviting our trust in Him on the basis of what He has done for us. Where there is no word from God, faith cannot be. Therefore, verbal revelation—that is to say, propositional revelation, the disclosure by God of truths about Himself—is no mere appendage to His redemptive activity, but a necessary part of it. This being so, the inspiring of an authoritative exposition of His redemptive acts in history ought to be seen as itself one of those redemptive acts, as necessary a link in the chain of His saving purposes as any of the events with which the exposition deals.

The need for verbal revelation appears most clearly when we consider the Person and work of Christ. His life and death was the clearest and fullest revelation of God that ever was or could be made. Yet it could never have been understood without explanation. Whoever could have *guessed*, without being told, that the man Jesus was God incarnate, that He had created the world in which He was crucified, that by dying a criminal's death He put away the sins of mankind, and that now, though gone from our sight, He lives for ever to bring penitent sinners to His Father? And who can come to faith in Christ if he knows none of this? No considerations could show more plainly the complete inability of man to 'make do' in his religion without a spoken word from God.

In fact, however, there is nothing of which the Bible is more sure than that God has from the first accompanied His redemptive acts with explanatory words—statements of fact about Himself and His purposes, warnings, commands, predictions, promises—and that it is in responding specifically to these divine words that obedience consists. Moses, the prophets, Christ, the apostles, all spoke God's words to men; and what they said took the form of statement and inference, argument and deduction.[1] God's word in their mouths was propositional in character. Christ and the apostles regularly appealed to Old Testament statements as providing a valid basis for inferences about God, and drew from them by the ordinary laws of grammar and logic conclusions which they put forward as truths revealed there—that the dead do not perish, that justification is by faith and not by works, that God is sovereign in saving mercy, and so forth.[2] Plainly, they regarded the Old Testament as propounding a body of doctrinal affirmations. And we have seen reasons already for regarding the New Testament as of the same nature as the Old. We conclude, therefore, that, if we are to follow Scripture's own account of itself, we are bound to say that whatever 'is either expressly set down in scripture, or by good and necessary consequence may be deduced from scripture'[3] must be regarded as a revealed truth. The Bible confronts us with the conception that the Word of God which it embodies consists of a system of truths, conveying to men real information from God about Himself.

Not that the text of Scripture is made up entirely of formal doctrinal statements; of course, it is not. The Bible is not a repository of isolated proof-texts, as the Mediæ-

[1] Bernard Ramm makes a striking observation on Christ's appeal to logic: 'With reference to logical forms our Lord used *analogy*, Luke xi. 13; *reductio ad absurdum*, Matt. xii. 26; *excluded middle*, Matt. xii. 30; *a fortiori*, Matt. xii. 1–8; *implication*, Matt. xii. 28; and law of *non-contradiction*, Luke vi. 39' (*The Pattern of Authority*, Eerdmans, 1957, p. 51). The list could be extended.

[2] Cf. Mk. xii. 26, 27; Gal. iii. 10–12; Rom. ix. 15–18, etc.

[3] Westminster Confession, I. vi.

vals, unconcerned about the literal sense of passages, were prone to think. Comparatively little of Scripture consists of systematic theological exposition; most of it is of a different order. Broadly speaking, the Bible is an interpretative record of sacred history. It reports God's words to Israel, and His dealings with them, down the ages. It includes biographies, meditations, prayers and praises, which show us how faith and unbelief, obedience and disobedience, temptation and conflict, work out in practice in human lives. It contains much imaginative matter—poetical, rhetorical, parabolic, visionary—which sets before our minds in a vivid, concrete and suggestive way great general principles, the formal statement of which has often to be sought in other contexts. In fact, Scripture is an organism, a complex, self-interpreting whole, its theology showing the meaning of the events and experiences which it records, and the events and experiences showing the outworking of the theology in actual life. All these items have their place in the total system of biblical truth.

It should be clear, therefore, that when we assert that what Scripture contains is a body of truths, embracing both matters of fact and general principles about God and man, and that these truths together constitute His Word, we are not prejudging the literary character of Scripture as a whole, or of any part of it. There is nothing in this position to cramp one's exegetical style, as some of the critics of Evangelicalism seem to fear. We do not suggest that every passage should be treated according to the same prearranged formula (as the Mediævals did by putting all texts through the same allegorical mincing-machine), but rather the very opposite—that we must recognize the complexity of Scripture, and do full justice to all the varied types of literary material which Scripture contains.

d. Infallibility and Inerrancy

Evangelicals are accustomed to speak of the Word of God as *infallible* and *inerrant*. The former term has a long pedigree; among the Reformers, Cranmer and Jewel spoke of God's Word as infallible,[1] and the Westminster Confession of 'the infallible truth' of Holy Scripture.[2] The latter, however, seems not to have been regularly used in this connection before the nineteenth century. Both have been so variously employed in theological discussion that they now bear no precise meaning at all. Terms which one cannot safely use without first stating what one does not mean by them are of little practical worth, and it might be argued that they, like the word 'fundamentalist', would be better dropped. Certainly, they are not essential for stating the evangelical view. If, however, they are construed in the sense intended by those who first applied them to Scripture, they express an important aspect of the approach to Scripture which we are outlining. For this reason, and because they have been misunderstood and misused in the present controversy, we shall briefly discuss them here.

'Infallible' denotes the quality of never deceiving or misleading, and so means 'wholly trustworthy and reliable'; 'inerrant' means 'wholly true'. Scripture is termed infallible and inerrant to express the conviction that all its teaching is the utterance of God 'who cannot lie',[3] whose word, once spoken, abides for ever,[4] and that therefore it may be trusted implicitly. This is just the conviction about Scripture which our Lord was expressing when He said: 'The scripture cannot be broken', and 'it is easier for heaven and earth to pass, than one tittle of the law to fail'.[5] God's Word is affirmed to be infallible because God Himself is infallible; the infallibility of Scripture is simply the infallibility of God speaking. What Scripture says is to be received as the infallible Word of

[1] See Cranmer, *Remains* (Parker Society), p. 19; Jewel, *Works* (P.S.), I. 80; cf. Ridley, *Works* (P.S.), p. 16, 'the infallible word of God'. The Latin equivalent is older still: Wycliffe speaks of Scripture as 'infallibilis . . . regula veritatis' (*De Veritate Sacrae Scriptural*, XXIV; written 1377–80), and Gerson (*ob.* 1429) in his *Tractatus de Examine Doctrinarum*, II. 17, describes Scripture as 'tanquam regula sufficiens et infallibilis pro regimine totius ecclesiastici corporis'. I owe these references to the Rev. R. T. Beckwith.

[2] I. v. [3] Tit. i. 2. [4] 1 Pet. i. 23–25; Ps. cxix. 89.

[5] Jn. x. 35; Lk. xvi. 17; cf. Mt. v. 18.

the infallible God, and to assert biblical inerrancy and infallibility is just to confess faith in (i) the divine origin of the Bible and (ii) the truthfulness and trustworthiness of God. The value of these terms is that they conserve the principle of biblical authority; for statements that are not absolutely true and reliable could not be absolutely authoritative.

The infallibility and inerrancy of biblical teaching does not, however, guarantee the infallibility and inerrancy of any interpretation, or interpreter, of that teaching; nor does the recognition of its qualities as the Word of God in any way prejudge the issue as to what Scripture does, in fact, assert. This can be determined only by careful Bible study. We must allow Scripture itself to define for us the scope and limits of its teaching. Too often the infallibility which belongs to the Word of God has been claimed for interpretations of Scripture which are, to say the least, uncertain and which make Scripture pronounce on subjects about which it does not itself claim to teach anything. The Bible is not an inspired 'Enquire Within Upon Everything'; it does not profess to give information about all branches of human knowledge in the way that Bradshaw professes to give information about all branches of British Railways. It claims in the broadest terms to teach all things necessary to salvation,[1] but it nowhere claims to give instruction in (for instance) any of the natural sciences, or in Greek and Hebrew grammar, and it would be an improper use of Scripture to treat it as making pronouncements on these matters.

We must draw a distinction between the subjects about which Scripture speaks and the terms in which it speaks of them. The biblical authors wrote of God's sovereignty over His world, and of man's experiences within that world, using such modes of speech about the natural order and human experience as were current in their days, and in a language that was common to themselves and their contemporaries. This is saying no more than that they wrote to be understood. Their picture of the world and things in it is not put forward as normative for later

[1] 2 Tim. iii. 16.

science, any more than their use of Hebrew and Greek is put forward as a perfect model for composition in these languages. They do not claim to teach either science or grammar.[1] Sometimes their grammar lapses; often the mental picture of the created order which their phraseology suggests to the twentieth-century mind differs from that of modern science;[2] but these facts do not bear on the inerrancy of the divine Word which the writers' conceptual and linguistic resources were being used to convey. This distinction between the content and the form of the written Word of God needs more discussion than we can give it here, but it seems clear enough in broad outline, although admittedly it is not always easily applied in particular cases. The question which the interpreter must

[1] Attempts to make Scripture teach science, either explicitly or by implication, have occasioned much fruitless labour, from post-Reformation days to the present time. For a review of some of these attempts, and a stimulating outline of the positive relation of Scripture to science, see R. Hooykaas, *Philosophia Libera: Christian Faith and the Freedom of Science* (Tyndale Press, 1957).

[2] This statement should perhaps be illustrated. It is often said that the Bible pictures the universe as like a house, of which the earth is the ground floor (standing on pillars, 1 Sa. ii. 8; and having foundations, Jb. xxxviii. 4), heaven the first floor (divided from the earth by a solid firmament, which acts as a ceiling for the earth, Gn. i. 8, and a floor for heaven, Ex. xxiv. 10), and Sheol, or Hades, the cellar (the pit into which the dead go down, Ps. lv. 15). Water is stored in heaven above the firmament (Gn. i. 7; Ps. cxlviii. 4) and rain starts and stops according as holes are opened and shut in the celestial roof (the windows of heaven, Gn. vii. 11). Again, it is often said that the Bible thinks of man's consciousness as diffused throughout his whole physical structure, so that each part of him is an independent centre of thought and feeling: thus, his bones speak (Ps. xxxv. 10), his bowels yearn (Gn. xliii. 30), his ear judges (Jb. xii. 11), his kidneys instruct him by night (Ps. xvi. 7), etc. It may be doubted whether these forms of speech were any more 'scientific' in character and intent than modern references to the sun rising, or light-headedness, or walking on air, or one's heart sinking into one's boots, would be. It is much likelier that they were simply standard pieces of imagery, which the writers utilized, and sometimes heightened for poetic effect, without a thought of what they would imply for cosmology and physiology if taken literally. And language means no more than it is used to mean. In any case, what the writers are concerned to tell us in the passages where they use these forms of speech is not the inner structure of the world and men, but the relation of both to God.

constantly ask is: what is being *asserted* in this passage? The more poetic, imaginative and symbolic the form in which the truth is presented, and the further the truth transcends our present experience and comprehension (as when Scripture tells us of life before the Fall, or in heaven), the harder it is to answer that question with exact precision. But the few passages in which it seems impossible to determine the limits of the symbolism with any finality (such as Gn. ii and iii, or Rev. xxi and xxii) are not typical of the Bible as a whole. In most passages, the use of the ordinary rules of exegesis enables us to determine accurately enough the limits of the intended assertions, and to distinguish them from linguistic forms which are simply vehicles for their communication and could be changed without altering their meaning.

This is just to say that the infallibility and inerrancy of Scripture are relative to the intended scope of the Word of God. Scripture provides instruction that is true and trustworthy, not on every conceivable subject, but simply on those subjects with which it claims to deal. We must allow Scripture itself to tell us what these are. The concepts of inerrancy and infallibility express one aspect of the conviction that the teaching of Scripture is the authoritative teaching of God, and call attention to the fact that it is always a wrong approach to treat anything that Scripture actually says as untrue or unreliable. But they are not hermeneutical concepts, and carry no implications as to the character or range of biblical teaching. Those matters can be settled only by honest and painstaking exegesis.

Dr. Hebert misunderstands the position of Evangelicals here. The 'rigid theory of the factual inerrancy of the Bible'[1] which he attributes to them involves, he supposes, not merely the recognition of its teaching as the Word of a truth-speaking God, but also the imposition upon it of a literalistic mode of interpretation which refuses to take account of the symbolic element in the telling of (for instance) the story of Adam and Eve. The concept of inerrancy, as he sees it, is thus an untheological concept,

[1] *Op. cit.*, p. 43.

and one which expresses an essentially untheological interest in vindicating the factual truthfulness of the Bible. This interest, he suggests, results from living in the twentieth century, and hence from being 'unconsciously dominated by the materialistic, intellectualistic view of truth which comes so readily to us in a scientific age'. It is because of this conditioning 'that it seems so plausible to think that if the Bible is true, it must be literally and factually true'. Hebert considers that 'a style of thinking which is alien to the Bible is being imposed forcibly upon it' by modern Evangelicals, and that their preoccupation with factuality inevitably leads to rather wooden and unedifying exposition of the text; he quotes the *New Bible Commentary*[1] as an example of this.[2] On this line of argument, we would make the following comments:

1. The idea that the doctrine of the inerrancy of the Word of God commits its adherents to a literalistic type of exegesis is wholly groundless. There is nothing inconsistent in recognizing that real events may be recorded in a highly symbolic manner, and Evangelicals do in fact recognize this. Dr. Hebert has evidently forgotten the passage which he himself quoted from the I.V.F. *New Bible Handbook* in which the use of symbolic modes of representation in the story of Adam and Eve is explicitly acknowledged.[3]

2. The evangelical insistence on the factuality of what Scripture presents as fact is neither new nor untheological. It goes back to the Reformation, when the allegorical method of exposition was abandoned in favour of the sounder principle that Scripture must be taken in its literal[4] sense. The way in which some have voiced and defended this conviction in recent years may reflect the influence of the modern scientific outlook; but the conviction itself derives, not from modern science, but from the Bible's own claim that what it tells is the truth, no less when it reports historical facts than when it states

[1] Inter-Varsity Fellowship, 1953.

[2] *Op. cit.*, pp. 96–98 and Chapter VII.

[3] *Op. cit.*, p. 40.

[4] For the meaning of this term, see pp. 102 ff. below.

theological principles. Dr. Hebert confesses it to be his faith (though he gives no satisfying proof) that Scripture errs in matters both of fact and of doctrine;[1] but he did not learn this faith from Christ and the apostles, who, as we saw, uniformly treated Scripture statements in both these categories as truths from God. The authority of Christ requires us to receive as God's Word all that the Bible asserts. No other attitude to biblical assertions is theologically warrantable; the untheological approach in this case is Hebert's own.

Maintaining the evangelical view of Scripture has always involved controversy, and the changing demands of controversy have naturally led to changes of emphasis in stating it. At the time of the Reformation, all the emphasis was laid on the truth of biblical doctrine, for it was only this that the then opponents of Evangelicalism —the church of Rome and the Socinian rationalists— would not face. For the past century, however, there has been as much need to insist on the truth of biblical testimony on matters of historical fact as on matters of theology, for liberal Protestants have regularly denied both. However, this increased emphasis on the factual truthfulness of the Word of God, to which Dr. Hebert calls attention, is not due to the materialistic influence of modern science, but to the characteristic form of modern heresy. So far from indicating a different approach to the Bible from that of the Reformers, as some suppose, it bears witness to an interest in maintaining the authority of the Bible which is identical with theirs.

3. While passing no judgment on modern evangelical standards of biblical exposition, we do not doubt that the approach to Scripture which we are outlining is far more likely to edify the Church than any modern version of the thesis that the written Word of God is true although it is false; that the teaching of Scripture is only roughly

[1] P. 139 and Chapter IV. His equation of the incompleteness of Old Testament revelation with error is an irrelevance. His repeated assumption of the legitimacy of rejecting, 'on critical grounds', such biblical affirmations as that Paul wrote the Pastoral Epistles begs the whole question of critical method; see Chapter VI below, and Appendix II, pp. 182 ff.

right, and that, though we ought to believe what we suppose the Bible means, we cannot believe all that it actually says. Only highly sophisticated persons could stomach such an approach in any case; but in this case it is simply a wrong approach. Perhaps, after all, the words 'inerrancy' and 'infallibility' have not yet outlived their usefulness as signposts to point to this fact.

III. THE INTERPRETATION OF SCRIPTURE[1]

We now come to the third part of this chapter, in which our aim will be to outline the biblical approach to biblical interpretation.

Scripture, as we have seen, is a many-sided interpretative record of an intricate cross-section of world history. The Word of God is an exceedingly complex unity. The different items and the various kinds of material which make it up—laws, promises, liturgies, genealogies, arguments, narratives, meditations, visions, aphorisms, homilies, parables and the rest—do not stand in Scripture as isolated fragments, but as parts of a whole. The exposition of them, therefore, involves exhibiting them in right relation both to the whole and to each other. God's Word is not presented in Scripture in the form of a theological system, but it admits of being stated in that form, and, indeed, requires to be so stated before we can properly grasp it—grasp it, that is, as a whole. Every text has its immediate context in the passage from which it comes, its broader context in the book to which it belongs, and its ultimate context in the Bible as a whole; and it needs to be rightly related to each of these contexts if its character, scope and significance is to be adequately understood.

An analogy may help here. A versatile writer with didactic intent, like Charles Williams or G. K. Chesterton, may express his thought in a variety of literary forms —poems, plays, novels, essays, critical and historical studies, as well as formal topical treatises. In such a case, it would be absurd to think any random sentence from

[1] For an excellent introduction to the discipline of biblical interpretation, see A. M. Stibbs, *Understanding God's Word* (Inter-Varsity Fellowship, 1950).

one of his works could safely be taken as expressing his whole mind on the subject with which it deals. The point of each sentence can be grasped only when one sees it in the context, both of the particular piece of work from which it comes, and of the writer's whole output. If we would understand the parts, our wisest course is to get to know the whole—or, at any rate, those parts of the whole which tell us in plain prose the writer's central ideas. These give us the key to all his work. Once we can see the main outlines of his thought and have grasped his general point of view, we are able to see the meaning of everything else—the point of his poems and the moral of his stories, and how the puzzling passages fit in with the rest. We may find that his message has a consistency hitherto unsuspected, and that elements in his thought which seemed contradictory are not really so at all. The task of interpreting the mind of God as expressed in His written Word is of the same order as this, and must be tackled in the same way. The beginner in Bible study often feels lost; he cannot at first grasp the Bible's over-all point of view, and so does not see the wood for trees. As his understanding increases, however, he becomes more able to discern the unity of the biblical message, and to see the place of each part in the whole.

a. Interpreting Scripture Literally

Scripture yields two basic principles for its own interpretation. The first is that the proper, natural sense of each passage (i.e., the intended sense of the writer) is to be taken as fundamental; the meaning of texts in their own contexts, and for their original readers, is the necessary starting-point for enquiry into their wider significance. In other words, Scripture statements must be interpreted in the light of the rules of grammar and discourse on the one hand, and of their own place in history on the other. This is what we should expect in the nature of the case, seeing that the biblical books originated as occasional documents addressed to contemporary audiences; and it is exemplified in the New Testament exposition of the Old, from which the fanciful allegorizing practised by

Philo and the Rabbis is strikingly absent. This is the much-misunderstood principle of interpreting Scripture *literally*. A glance at its history will be the quickest way of clearing up the confusion.

The Mediæval exegetes, following Origen, regarded the 'literal' sense of Scripture as unimportant and unedifying. They attributed to each biblical statement three further senses, or levels of meaning, each of which was in a broad sense allegorical: the 'moral' or 'tropological' (from which one learned rules of conduct), the 'allegorical' proper (from which one learned articles of faith), and the 'anagogical' (from which one learned of the invisible realities of heaven). Thus, it was held that the term 'Jerusalem' in Scripture, while denoting 'literally' a city in Palestine, also referred 'morally' to civil society, 'allegorically' to the Church, and 'anagogically' to heaven, every time that it occurred. Only the three allegorical senses, the Mediævals held, were worth a theologian's study; the literal record had no value save as a vehicle of figurative meaning. Mediæval exegesis was thus exclusively mystical, not historical at all; biblical facts were made simply a jumping-off ground for theological fancies, and thus spiritualized away. Against this the Reformers protested, insisting that the literal, or intended, sense of Scripture was the sole guide to God's meaning. They were at pains to point out, however, that 'literalism' of this sort, so far from precluding the recognition of figures of speech where Scripture employs them, actually demands it. William Tyndale's statement of their position may be quoted as typical: 'Thou shalt understand, therefore, that the scripture hath but one sense, which is the literal sense. And that literal sense is the root and ground of all, and the anchor that never faileth, whereunto if thou cleave, thou canst never err or go out of the way. And if thou leave the literal sense, thou canst not but go out of the way. Nevertheless, the scripture uses proverbs, similitudes, riddles, or allegories, as all other speeches do; but that which the proverb, similitude, riddle or allegory signifieth, is ever the literal sense, which thou must seek out diligently.'

Tyndale castigates the Scholastics for misapplying 2

Cor. iii. 6 to support their thesis that 'the literal sense . . . is hurtful, and noisome, and killeth the soul', and only spiritualizing does any good; and he replaces their distinction between the literal and spiritual senses by an equation which reflects Jn. vi. 63 : 'God is a Spirit, and all his words are spiritual. His literal sense is spiritual . . . if thou have eyes of God to see the right meaning of the text, and whereunto the Scripture pertaineth, and the final end and cause thereof.'[1] Fanciful spiritualizing, so far from yielding God's meaning, actually obscured it. The literal sense is itself the spiritual sense, coming from God and leading to Him.

This 'literalism' is founded on respect for the biblical forms of speech; it is essentially a protest against the arbitrary imposition of inapplicable literary categories on scriptural statements. It is this 'literalism' that present-day Evangelicals profess. But to read all Scripture narratives as if they were eye-witness reports in a modern newspaper, and to ignore the poetic and imaginative form in which they are sometimes couched, would be no less a violation of the canons of evangelical 'literalism' than the allegorizing of the Scholastics was; and this sort of 'literalism' Evangelicals repudiate. It would be better to call such exegesis 'literalistic' rather than 'literal', so as to avoid confusing two very different things.[2]

The modern outcry against evangelical 'literalism' seems to come from those who want leave to sit loose to biblical categories and treat the biblical records of certain events as myths, or parables—non-factual symbols of spiritual states and experiences. Many would view the story of the fall, for instance, merely as a picture of the present sinful condition of each man, and that of the virgin birth as merely expressing the thought of Christ's

[1] Tyndale, *Works* (Parker Society), I. 304 ff. The judicious Richard Hooker was making the same point when he wrote: 'I hold it for a most infallible rule in the exposition of Scripture, that when a literal construction will stand, the furthest from the literal is commonly the worst' (*Laws of Ecclesiastical Polity*, V. lix. 2).

[2] For a good short review of some of the narrative and didactic forms of Scripture, see J. Stafford Wright, *Interpreting the Bible* (Inter-Varsity Fellowship, 1955).

superhuman character. Such ideas are attempts to cut the knot tied by the modern critical denial that these events really happened, and to find a way of saying that, though the stories are 'literally' false, yet they remain 'spiritually' true and valuable. Those who take this line upbraid Evangelicals for being insensitive to the presence of symbolism in Scripture. But this is not the issue. There is a world of difference between recognizing that a real event (the fall, say) may be symbolically portrayed, as Evangelicals do, and arguing, as these persons do, that because the fall is symbolically portrayed, it need not be regarded as a real event at all, but is merely a picture of something else. In opposing such inferences, Evangelicals are contending, not for a literalistic view, but for the very principles of biblical literalism which we have already stated—that we must respect the literary categories of Scripture, and take seriously the historical character of the Bible story. We may not turn narratives which clearly purport to record actual events into mere symbols of human experience at our will; still less may we do so (as has been done) in the name of biblical theology! We must allow Scripture to tell us its own literary character, and be willing to receive it as what it claims to be.

It may be thought that the historic Protestant use of the word 'literal' which we have here been concerned to explain is so unnatural on modern lips, and that such a weight of misleading association now attaches to the term, that it would be wisest to drop it altogether. We argued earlier that the word 'fundamentalist' should be dropped, as having become a barrier to mutual understanding, and the case may well be the same here. We do not contend for words. We are not bound to cling to 'literal' as part of our theological vocabulary; it is not itself a biblical term, and we can state evangelical principles of interpretation without recourse to it (as, indeed, we did in the opening sentences of this section);[1] and perhaps it is better that we should. If we do abandon the word, however, we must not abandon the principle which it enshrines: namely, that Scripture is to be interpreted in its natural, intended

[1] P. 102 above.

sense, and theological predilections must not be allowed to divert us from loyalty to what the text actually asserts.

b. Interpreting Scripture by Scripture

The second basic principle of interpretation is that Scripture must interpret Scripture; the scope and significance of one passage is to be brought out by relating it to others. Our Lord gave an example of this when he used Gn. ii. 24 to show that Moses' law of divorce was no more than a temporary concession to human hard-heartedness.[1] The Reformers termed this principle the analogy of Scripture; the Westminster Confession states it thus: 'The infallible rule of interpretation of scripture is the scripture itself; and therefore, when there is a question about the true and full sense of any scripture, it must be searched and known by other places that speak more clearly.'[2] This is so in the nature of the case, since the various inspired books are dealing with complementary aspects of the same subject. The rule means that we must give ourselves in Bible study to following out the unities, cross-references and topical links which Scripture provides. Kings and Chronicles throw light on each other; so do the prophets and the history books of the Old Testament; so do the Synoptic Gospels and John; so do the four Gospels and the Epistles; so, indeed, do the Old Testament as a whole and the New. And there is one book in the New Testament which links up with almost everything that the Bible contains: that is the Epistle to the Romans, of which Calvin justly wrote in the Epistle prefacing his commentary on it: 'If a man understands it, he has a sure road opened for him to the understanding of the whole Scripture.' In Romans, Paul brings together and sets out in systematic relation all the great themes of the Bible—sin, law, judgment, faith, works, grace, justification, sanctification, election, the plan of salvation, the work of Christ, the work of the Spirit, the Christian hope, the nature and life of the Church, the place of Jew and Gentile in the purposes of God, the philosophy of Church and of world history, the meaning and message of the Old Testament, the duties of

[1] Mt. xix. 3–8, dealing with Dt. xxiv. 1. [2] I. ix.

Christian citizenship, the principles of personal piety and ethics. From the vantage-point given by Romans, the whole landscape of the Bible is open to view, and the broad relation of the parts to the whole becomes plain. The study of Romans is the fittest starting-point for biblical interpretation and theology.

c. Problems and Difficulties

The scientific study of Scripture is a complicated and exacting task. The biblical languages have their own distinctive idioms and thought-forms. Each writer has his own habits of mind, vocabulary, outlook and interests. Each book has its own character, and is written according to stylistic conventions which it is not always easy to see. Each book has its own historical and theological background, and must be interpreted against that background; thus, we should not look in the Old Testament for clear statements about the Trinity, or the believer's hope of a future life, for these things were not fully revealed till Christ came. All these factors must be borne in mind, or we shall misinterpret Scripture.

This does not mean that only trained scholars can study the Bible to any profit. Its central message is so plainly stated in the text that the most unlearned of those who have ears to hear and eyes to see can understand it. 'The unfolding of thy words gives light; it imparts understanding to the simple.'[1] The technicalities of scholarship may be out of the ordinary Bible-reader's reach, but none the less he can, with God's blessing, grasp all the main truths of God's message. 'Those things which are necessary to be known, believed, and observed, for salvation, are so clearly propounded and opened in some place of scripture or other, that not only the learned, but the unlearned, in a due use of the ordinary means, may attain unto a sufficient understanding of them.' [2] It is only over secondary matters that problems arise. Here, however, ignorance of the background of biblical statements and allusions, coupled (no doubt) with failure to enter adequately into

[1] Ps. cxix. 130, RSV.

[2] Westminster Confession, I. vii.

the writers' minds,[1] leave us on occasion in doubt as to what texts mean, and how they fit in with other texts and with the rest of the Word of God. But these uncertainties affect only the outer fringes of the biblical revelation. And in fact, this class of problem steadily yields to patient study as our knowledge grows. As in all scientific enquiry, however, the solution of one problem raises another and we have no reason to expect that all the problems that crop up in biblical exposition will ever be completely solved in this world.

An idea that persistently haunts some people is that the presence in Scripture of passages which are hard to harmonize is an argument against regarding it as God's Word written in the sense we have explained, and that one is not entitled so to regard it until one has first reconciled all the seeming discrepancies to one's own satisfaction. If this were right, every apparent contradiction would be a valid reason for doubting the truth of the biblical doctrine of Scripture. But the idea rests on a confusion. Christians are bound to receive the Bible as God's Word written on the authority of Christ, not because they can prove it such by independent enquiry, but because as disciples they trust their divine Teacher. We have pointed out already that no article of Christian faith admits of full rational demonstration as, say, geometrical theorems do; all the great biblical doctrines—the Trinity, the incarnation, the atonement, the work of the Spirit in man, the resurrection of the body and the renewal of the creation—are partly mysterious, and raise problems for our minds that are at present insoluble. The doctrine of Scripture is no exception to this rule. But that should not daunt, nor even surprise us; for it is the very nature of Christian faith to believe, on the authority of God, truths which may neither be rationally demonstrated nor exhaustively understood. We must remember that God does not tell us everything about His acts and purposes, nor put us in a position to work them all out for ourselves. We shall not reach right views about the things of God by backing our independent

[1] Cf. 2 Pet. iii. 16.

judgment, but only by taking His word. We are wholly dependent on Him for our knowledge of His ways.

God, then, does not profess to answer in Scripture all the questions that we, in our boundless curiosity, would like to ask about Scripture. He tells us merely as much as He sees we need to know as a basis for our life of faith. And He leaves unsolved some of the problems raised by what He tells us, in order to teach us a humble trust in His veracity. The question, therefore, that we must ask ourselves when faced with these puzzles is not, is it reasonable to imagine that this is so? but, is it reasonable to accept God's assurance that this is so? Is it reasonable to take God's word and believe that He has spoken the truth, even though I cannot fully comprehend what He has said? The question carries its own answer. We should not abandon faith in anything that God has taught us merely because we cannot solve all the problems which it raises. Our own intellectual competence is not the test and measure of divine truth. It is not for us to stop believing because we lack understanding, or to postpone believing till we can get understanding, but to believe in order that we may understand; as Augustine said, 'unless you believe, you will not understand.' Faith first, sight afterwards, is God's order, not *vice versa*; and the proof of the sincerity of our faith is our willingness to have it so. Therefore, just as we should not hesitate to commit ourselves to faith in the Trinity although we do not know how one God can be three Persons, nor to faith in the incarnation, although we do not know how the divine and human natures combined in the Person of Christ, so we should not hesitate to commit ourselves to faith in Scripture as the infallible Word of the infallible God, even though we cannot solve all the puzzles, nor reconcile all the apparent contradictions, with which in our present state of knowledge it confronts us. On all these articles of faith we have God's positive assurance; and that should be enough.

Accordingly, our methods of interpreting Scripture must be such as express faith in its truth and consistency as God's Word. Our approach must be harmonistic; for we know at the outset that God's utterance is not self-contradictory. Article XX of the Church of England lays down that it is not lawful for the Church so to 'expound one place of Scripture, that it be repugnant to another'; no more is it lawful for any individual exegete. Not that we should adopt strained and artificial expedients for harmonizing; this will neither glorify God nor edify us. What we cannot harmonize by a natural and plausible hypothesis is best left unharmonized, with a frank admission that in our present state of knowledge we do not see how these apparent discrepancies should be resolved. We may not, with the heretic Marcion and some modern Liberals, 'criticize the Bible by the Bible', singling out some parts of Scripture as the authentic Word of God and denying the divine character of the rest because it seems to say something different from the parts approved; instead, we should confess the divine origin of all the Scriptures, and be guided in interpreting them by Augustine's axiom: 'I do not doubt that their authors therein made no mistake and set forth nothing that might mislead. If in one of these books I stumble across something which seems opposed to the truth, I have no hesitation in saying that either my copy is faulty, or the translator has not fully grasped what was said' (Augustine read Scripture in Latin), 'or else I myself have not fully understood.'[1] We must base our study of Scripture on the assumption that governed the New Testament men in their study of the Old—that God's revealed truth is a consistent unity, and any disharmony between part and part is only apparent, not real.

d. The Holy Spirit as Interpreter

One final point concerning interpretation remains to be made. Scripture tells us that if we are to understand Scripture we need, over and above right rules, personal insight into spiritual things. Scripture sets before us spiritual truths—truths, that is, about God, and about created things in relation to God; and to grasp spiritual truths requires spiritual receptiveness. But no man has this by nature. 'The natural man receiveth not the things

[1] *Ep.* lxxxii.

of the Spirit of God: for they are foolishness unto him: neither can he know them, because they are spiritually discerned.'[1] The habit of mind which enslaves the natural man, Paul tells us, is to set up his own 'wisdom' and make it ultimate, and so he is compelled to dismiss as foolishness all that does not accord with it. Without spiritual enlightenment, he will never be able to see the foolishness of his own wisdom, nor the wisdom of the 'foolishness of God'[2] proclaimed in the gospel; hence he will never forsake the one for the other. Our Lord confirms this view of man. His repeated diagnosis of the unbelieving Pharisees was that they were *blind*, lacking the capacity to perceive spiritual realities;[3] and He regarded spiritual perception, where He found it, as a supernatural gift from God.[4]

Now, the Holy Spirit has been sent to the Church as its Teacher, to guide Christians into truth, to make them wise unto salvation, to testify to them of Christ and to glorify Him thereby.[5] To the apostles, He came to remind them of Christ's teaching, to show them its meaning, to add further revelation to it, and so to equip them to witness to all about their Lord.[6] To other men, He comes to make them partakers of the apostolic faith through the apostolic word. Paul indicates the permanent relation between the Spirit, the apostles' word and the rest of the Church in 1 Cor. ii. 10–16. The Spirit, he says, gave the apostles understanding of the gospel: 'we have received, not the spirit of the world, but the spirit which is of God; that we might know the things that are freely given to us of God'; 'God hath revealed them unto us by his Spirit,' Now the Spirit inspires and empowers their proclamation of these things to other men: 'which things we speak, not in the words which man's wisdom teacheth, but which the Holy Ghost teacheth'; Paul preaches, and knows that he preaches, 'in demonstration of the Spirit and of power'.[7] And 'he that is spiritual'—he in whom the Spirit abides to give understanding—discerns the meaning of the message

[1] 1 Cor. ii. 14. [2] 1 Cor. i. 25; see the whole passage, i. 18 ff.
[3] Mt. xv. 14, xxiii. 16, 17, 19, 26; Jn. ix. 39–41.
[4] Mt. xi. 25, xvi. 17. [5] Jn. xiv. 26, xv. 26, xvi. 13, 14.
[6] Jn. xiv. 26, xvi. 12, 13, xvii. 20. [7] 1 Cor. ii. 4.

and receives it as the testimony of God. This applies no less to the apostolic word written than to the apostolic word preached; and no more to the apostolic writings than to the rest of the written Word of God. The Spirit, who was its author, is also its interpreter, and such understanding of it as men gain is His gift.

Not that the Spirit's presence in men's hearts makes patient study of the text unnecessary. The Spirit is not given to make Bible study needless, but to make it effective. Nor can anything in Scripture mean anything when the Spirit interprets. The Spirit is not the prompter of fanciful spiritualizing, or of applications of texts out of their contexts on the basis of accidental associations of words. The only meaning to which He bears witness is that which each text actually has in the organism of Scripture; such witness as is borne to other meanings is borne by other spirits. But without the Spirit's help there can be no grasp of the message of Scripture, no conviction of the truth of Scripture, and no faith in the God of Scripture. Without the Spirit, nothing is possible but spiritual blindness and unbelief.

It follows that the Christian must approach the study of Scripture in humble dependence on the Holy Spirit, sure that he can learn from it nothing of spiritual significance unless he is taught of God. Confidence in one's own powers of discernment is an effective barrier to spiritual understanding. The self-confidence of nineteenth-century critical scholarship was reflected in its slogan that the Bible must be read like any other book; but the Bible is more than a merely human book, and understanding it involves more than appreciating its merely human characteristics. God's book does not yield up its secrets to those who will not be taught of the Spirit. Our God-given textbook is a closed book till our God-given Teacher opens it to us.

A century of criticism has certainly thrown some light on the human side of the Bible—its style, language, composition, history and culture; but whether it has brought the Church a better understanding of its divine message than Evangelicals of two, three and four hundred years ago possessed is more than doubtful. It is not at all clear that we today comprehend the plan of salvation, the doctrines of sin, election, atonement, justification, new birth and sanctification, the life of faith, the duties of churchmanship and the meaning of Church history, more clearly than did the Reformers, or the Puritans, or the leaders of the eighteenth-century revival. When it is claimed that modern criticism has greatly advanced our understanding of the Bible, the reply must be that it depends upon what is meant by the Bible; criticism has thrown much light on the human features of Scripture, but it has not greatly furthered our knowledge of the Word of God. Indeed, it seems truer to say that its effect to date has been rather to foster ignorance of the Word of God; for by concentrating on the human side of Scripture it has blurred the Church's awareness of the divine character of scriptural teaching, and by questioning biblical statements in the name of scholarship it has shaken confidence in the value of personal Bible study. Hence, just as the Mediævals tended to equate Church tradition with the Word of God, so modern Protestants tend to equate the words of scholars with the Word of God. We have fallen into the habit of accepting their pronouncements at second hand without invoking the Spirit's help to search Scripture and see, not merely whether what they say is so (in so far as the lay Bible student is qualified to judge this), but also—often more important—whether God's Word does not deal with more than the limited number of topics with which scholars at any one time are concerned. The result of this negligence is widespread ignorance among Churchmen as to what Scripture actually says. So it always is when the Church forgets how to search the Scriptures acknowledging its own blindness and looking to God's Spirit to teach it God's truth. There is no more urgent need today than that the Church should humble itself to learn this lesson once more.

We have now presented in positive outline the biblical approach to Scripture. Its text is word for word God-given; its message is an organic unity, the infallible Word of an infallible God, a web of revealed truths centred upon Christ; it must be interpreted in its natural sense, on the assumption of its inner harmony; and its meaning can be grasped only by those who humbly seek and gladly receive the help of the Holy Spirit.

CHAPTER V

FAITH

The Holy Spirit is no Sceptic, and the things He has written in our hearts are not doubts or opinions, but assertions—surer and more certain than sense or life itself.

LUTHER TO ERASMUS

All thy children shall be taught of the Lord; and great shall be the peace of thy children.

ISAIAH liv. 13

Now faith is . . . the conviction of things not seen.

HEBREWS xi. 1, RSV

WE have now outlined the view of the nature of Scripture as a revelation, and of its intended function as an authority, which the Bible sets before us. The next step in our argument is to show that this view is to be received by faith. It is not necessary for our present purpose to enter into a full discussion of the nature of saving faith, as the act and attitude of self-committal whereby the convicted sinner, humbled to see his need and his natural inability even to trust, casts himself in the God-given confidence of self-despair on the mercy of Christ Jesus. This is not directly in dispute, and it seems that some anti-fundamentalists would be in broad agreement with us about it. We shall confine our discussion to the intellectual and cognitive aspect of faith, as, in general, an activity of apprehending divine revelation for what it is, and, more particularly, of receiving and revering the Bible as the Word of God.

Let us begin by asking: what is the nature of faith? 'Trust' is the general idea that the word conveys. The specific character of trust, however, is determined in each case by its object. Trust in one's wife, one's judgment or one's lucky star are three different things, though each is an instance of the same generic attitude of reliance. The confidence which we repose in men is something different from that which we place in things, and the faith which we rest in God is a form of reliance distinct from either. The difference is accounted for in each case by the nature of the object trusted. The difference between faith in God and all other attitudes of trust derives from the unique character of its object—the Creator who declares mercy to His sinful creatures. Scripture speaks of this faith as having, strictly speaking, a twofold object: the words of God, and the God who speaks them—God's truth, and God's Person. And the first is evidently basic to the second. One must know something about God before one can know Him. Truth is fundamental to trust. It is true, as is often insisted, that biblical faith is more than *fides* (credence); its object is something more than a body of sound doctrine; there is no faith, in the biblical sense, without *fiducia*, personal trust in the living God through the living Christ. But it is equally true that faith is not less than credence. It is a false antithesis, and a very silly one, to oppose faith as trust to faith as credence; for the Christian trusts the Christ of the gospel because he believes that what the gospel says of Him is right. Did he not believe the gospel, he would have no grounds for such trust, and could not rationally exercise it. We have seen already with what emphasis the New Testament insists that there can be no faith without prior knowledge and belief of the truth of the gospel.[1] It does not acknowledge as 'faith' any religious attitude of mind or heart based on other beliefs, such as is found in pagan religions. Belief of what is not God's truth will prompt the rejection of what is; and the Bible name for that (however religiously done) is unbelief.

What is the proper basis for credence? On what ground should articles of faith be believed? As we can see from what has been said, it is not rational demonstration. Truths about God, by their very nature, can be only partly grasped by man, and cannot therefore be demonstratively proved; for such proof is only possible in principle on the basis of an exhaustive understanding of its object. Articles of faith, then, are not dictates of reason.

[1] See pp. 42 f. above.

They are not in themselves unreasonable, but they are above reason; they terminate in mysteries which the human mind can express only as paradoxes—three Persons in one God, one Person in two natures, man both free and controlled, and so on. Reasoning may prepare the mind for faith in these truths, by showing their meaning and biblical basis, their congruity with the total biblical outlook and the known facts of life, and the weakness of objections made to them; but reasoning alone cannot produce faith, for faith goes further than reason could take it. Reasoning could at best suggest only probability; but the nature of faith is to be certain. Any measure of doubt or uncertainty is not a degree of faith, but an assault upon it. Faith, therefore, must rest on something more sure than an inference of probability.

Once more, then, we ask: on what account ought articles of faith to be received? On what basis may we rationally urge men to believe them? If we should say 'Believe them, because Scripture teaches them', that (though right in itself) would be an incomplete answer, because it would at once prompt the further question: 'On what grounds should we receive biblical doctrines as true?' If we should say 'Believe them, because Jesus and the apostles taught them', that (though also right) would still be an incomplete answer, because we should then be asked: 'What grounds are there for receiving their teaching as true?' In either case, our original question would merely be pushed one stage further back. Scripture answers it by resolving the ground of faith, formally, into the veracity of God and, materially, into the divine origin of the propositions put forward for belief. The proper basis for believing is, on the one hand, the acknowledgment that God speaks only truth and, on the other, the recognition of what is proposed as something which He Himself has said. Articles of faith are just truths for which God is perceived to have vouched. It is fundamental to the nature of faith to take God's word for things; acceptance on the authority of God is the biblical analysis of faith on its intellectual side. The first manifestation of faith is cognitive: it appears in the recognition of affirmations made by men—prophets, apostles, the man Christ Jesus, any biblical writer—as truths uttered by God. Faith apprehends their testimony to God as being God's own testimony to Himself, and receives and responds to it as such.[1]

The ground of faith, then, is the recognition of man's word as God's word. How does it come about? Through the work of the Holy Spirit, opening and enlightening the 'eyes' of the mind (which is where faith begins) so that man 'sees' and knows the divine source and spiritual meaning of the message that confronts him.[2] This illumination is the direct ground of all faith's grasp of the things of God. Scripture presents it as the last stage in the complex process of revelation. Having disclosed Himself objectively in history, in His incarnate Son, and in His written, scriptural Word, God now enlightens men subjectively in experience, so that they apprehend His self-disclosure for what it is.[3] Thus He causes them to know Him, and His end in revelation is achieved.

Not that the divine character of the Word which mediates His self-disclosure to men is not objectively clear. Scripture conceives of the divine character of revealed truth as something which evidences itself to the sound mind as clearly as do light and colour to the normal eye. But man's mental 'eyes' are blind through sin, and he can discern no part of God's truth till the Spirit opens them.[4] Inner illumination, leading directly as it does to a deep, inescapable conviction, is thus fundamental to the Spirit's work as a teacher. It was of this that John spoke when, writing to reassure his readers that it was they and not the Gnostic seceders who knew God and had eternal life, he appealed to the 'anointing from the Holy One' which 'teacheth you concerning all things', and declared: 'The Son of God is come, and hath given us an understanding, that we know him that is true.'[5] Else-

[1] 1 Thes. ii. 13; 2 Thes. ii. 11, 12; cf. Rom. ii. 8; 2 Tim. ii. 25; Tit. i. 1; 1 Pet. i. 22, etc.

[2] Jn. iii. 3; 1 Cor. ii. 14, 15; 2 Cor. iv. 6; Eph. i. 18, etc.

[3] Cf. Mt. xi. 25, xvi. 17; Gal. i. 16.

[4] 2 Cor. iv. 4; Eph. iv. 18.

[5] 1 Jn. ii. 20, 27, v. 20.

where, he says: 'the Spirit . . . beareth witness' to Christ, referring, apparently, to this same inner enlightenment.[1] Historic Protestantism, interpreting the text in this sense, has regularly described this part of the Spirit's ministry as His witness to divine truth. It is a healing of spiritual faculties, a restoring to man of a permanent receptiveness towards divine things, a giving and sustaining of power to recognize and receive divine utterances for what they are. It is given in conjunction with the hearing or reading of such utterances, and the immediate fruit of it is an inescapable awareness of their divine origin and authority.

And when this starts to happen, faith is being born. Faith begins with the according of credence to revealed truths, not as popular, or probable, human opinions, but as words uttered by the Creator, and uttered, not only to mankind in general, but to the individual soul in particular. The personal application of the Christian message is realized as the Spirit convinces of sin, of righteousness and of judgment. Credence then finds its fulfilment in trust as the sinner is enabled to cast himself on Christ the Mediator and to close with Him as Saviour. And the life of faith which he lives from then on is one of continuing credence and trust.

Now, all the divine utterances which faith apprehends are in fact scriptural affirmations; for there are no words of God spoken to us at all today except the words of Scripture (direct revelations having now ceased). Conversely, all scriptural affirmations are in fact divine utterances, and are through the Spirit apprehended as such by faith. But among the affirmations of Scripture is the biblical doctrine of Scripture which we have surveyed; and one effect of the Spirit's witnessing action is to make men bow to this doctrine. The case is just the same as with any other article of faith. The scriptural witness to this doctrine is full and clear; writer after writer affirms the divine origin and authority of the written Word, and Christ, as we saw, based Christianity upon it. Yet it is not credited by the Church apart from spiritual illumina-

[1] 1 Jn. v. 7.

tion. As the Westminster Confession puts it: 'We may be moved and induced by the testimony of the Church to a high and reverend esteem of the holy scripture, and the heavenliness of the matter, the efficacy of the doctrine, the majesty of the style, the consent of all the parts, the scope of the whole (which is to give all glory to God), the full discovery it makes of the only way of man's salvation, the many other incomparable excellencies, and the entire perfection thereof, are arguments whereby it doth abundantly evidence itself to be the word of God; yet notwithstanding our full persuasion and assurance of the infallible truth, and divine authority thereof, is from the inward work of the Holy Spirit, bearing witness by and with the words in our hearts.'[1] This witness is not, as is sometimes supposed, an inner voice, or a mystical experience, or that sense of being gripped and searched by particular passages of which Coleridge spoke when he said: 'Whatever *finds* me, bears witness of itself that it has proceeded from a Holy Spirit.' It is, in fact, the same witness that we have described already: that enlightening action which is the root of all faith, inasmuch as it alone enables sinners to discern and respond to revealed truth as such. The specific convictions to which it leads are those to which Scripture itself bears witness—in this case, that Scripture is from God, and that all it says is to be received as His Word. The effect of this witness is thus the self-authentication of Scripture to the Christian's conscience. We conclude that, where there is faith in Christ, and the Bible is known and read at all, there also, more or less explicit, is faith in Scripture as God's written Word.

The classic statement on the Spirit's witness in relation to Scripture is that of Calvin.[2] Having rejected the idea that faith in the authoritative truth of Scripture should rest on the witness of an authoritative Church, Calvin lays down the following principle:

'They who labour to raise up a firm faith in Scripture by arguing are acting absurdly. . . . For as God alone is competent to bear witness of himself in his own word, so that word will not find credence in the hearts of men

[1] I. v. [2] *Institutes of the Christian Religion*, I. vii.

till it is sealed upon them by the inner witness of the Spirit. The same Spirit, therefore, who spoke by the mouth of the prophets, must make his way into our hearts to assure us that they faithfully delivered that which was divinely entrusted to them. . . . Some good men are disconcerted that, while irreligious persons raise objections with impunity against the word of God, no clear proof of it is ready to hand; as if it were not the case that the Spirit is called a seal and an earnest to confirm the faith of the godly just because, until he enlightens their minds, they waver amid a multitude of doubts.' And he proceeds:

'Let this, then, remain fixed: that those whom the Holy Spirit inwardly teaches firmly acquiesce in Scripture; and that Scripture is in truth authoritative in itself (*autopiston*), nor is it right for it to be made subject to demonstration and arguments; but that it owes the sense of certainty which we ought to have about it to the witness of the Spirit. For though it commands reverence of itself, by its own majestic character, it only makes a serious impact on us when it is sealed on our heart by the Spirit. Enlightened by his power, therefore, we do not believe that Scripture is from God on the basis of either our own judgment, or another's; but, with a certainty that transcends human judgment, we are unshakably convinced—as though we saw God himself present in it—that it has come to us, by the ministry of men, from God's very mouth. We ask not for proofs or probabilities on which our judgment may rest, but we subject our mind and judgment to it, as something beyond reach of our assessing.'

Such, says Calvin, is the conviction of all who have the Spirit: 'I say nothing more than every believer experiences in himself, though my words fall far short of an adequate account of the reality.' Just as the Spirit teaches all Christians to receive as authoritative articles of faith the doctrines which the Scriptures assert, so He teaches them to regard as an authoritative source of doctrine the Scriptures which assert them.

Nor is this view peculiar to Calvin. Professor Alan

Richardson insists with justice that Calvin here is simply crystallizing something that has always been part of the Church's faith. 'His teaching that the Christian's recognition of the authority of the Bible is due to the working of the Holy Spirit in his heart gives classical expression to a doctrine which has been believed by Christians in every century. . . . It is a doctrine of the whole Church . . . one for which support could be found in the writings of practically every leading theologian of the Church in every age.'[1] Without claiming to understand all that Scripture contains, nor to have been 'found' in Coleridge's sense by every single text, the Church has from the first professed to receive the Bible's testimony to its own divine origin, and believed that it was the Spirit who taught it to do so. The doctrine of the Spirit's witness to Scripture, thus understood, is and always was part of the catholic faith.

Now, it is this catholic doctrine that explains the certainty and confidence of Evangelicals as to the divine truth and trustworthiness of the Bible. Some, as we saw, think this robust confidence unwarrantable, and explain it as a sociological phenomenon—a piece of wishful thinking prompted by the craving for certainty which we all feel, adolescents especially, in our unsettled and rootless age. Evangelicals, it is said, cling to the idea of biblical infallibility as drowning men cling to a straw—not because it is worthy of their trust, but because they want something to cling to and there is nothing else within reach. We can now see how perverse a misunderstanding this is. The evangelical certainty of the trustworthiness and authority of Scripture is of exactly the same sort, and rests on exactly the same basis, as the Church's certainty of the Trinity, or the incarnation, or any other catholic doctrine. God has declared it; Scripture embodies it; the Spirit exhibits it to believers; and they humbly receive it, as they are bound to do. It is not optional for Christians to sit loose to what God has said, and treat questions which He has closed as if they were still open. The truth is that the evangelical doctrine of Scripture is

[1] *Christian Apologetics* (S.C.M., 1947), pp. 212 ff.

an article of the catholic faith, and the evangelical confidence in its truth is part of the Church's Spirit-given assurance of faith. It is strange that those who think Evangelicals odd for being sure of the biblical doctrine of Scripture do not see that so-called 'biblical theologians' who are not sure of it are much more odd. It is stranger still that those who accuse Evangelicals of 'heresy' for their view of the Bible should fail to grasp that it is not Evangelicals, but they themselves who have parted company with the historic catholic faith. One recalls the fond mother who watched the parade and concluded that all were out of step except her Johnny.

It will be asked why, if the whole Church does in fact experience the witness of the Spirit to Scripture, any Christian should ever deviate from the Bible's view of itself. The same question arises in connection with unscriptural views of any doctrine. It does not seem hard to answer. Christians fall into mental error, partly through mistaking or overlooking what Scripture teaches, partly through having their minds prepossessed with unbiblical notions so that they cannot take scriptural statements seriously. All heresy begins so. In this case, our issue is with the liberal approach to Scripture, and we hope to show in the next chapters that this has been determined by an unbiblical view of the Christian use of reason. Meanwhile, we would point out that, when false principles possess the minds of Christian men, they go against their own deepest spiritual instincts. Unscriptural ideas in our theology are like germs in our system. They tend only to weaken and destroy life, and their effect is always damaging, more or less. But they provoke resistance. Heretical notions may occupy Christian men's heads, leading to error of thought and practice and spiritual impoverishment; but these notions cannot wholly control their hearts. As regenerate men, it is their nature to be better than the unscriptural parts of their creed would allow. Hence they are inconsistent; it is good that they are. In this case, Christians in the liberal camp have adopted a position which logically makes reason, and not Scripture, their final authority. But, just because they are

Christians and have the witness of the Spirit, it is not in their nature to follow this anti-Christian principle to its logical conclusion—which would be to dismiss as incredible all that is incomprehensible, and so to deny the whole Christian faith. Regenerate men can never do that. Hence we find that they are in practice inconsistent. Though they evade the Bible's testimony to itself, they accept at its face value its testimony to other articles of faith. Radicals who query the truth and worth of much of Scripture are yet devout Bible-readers and vigorous preachers of the gospel, and that from texts whose credit they would deny in the lecture-room. Theological students sometimes wonder at the *volte-face* that takes place when their lecturers enter the pulpit! The impression thus given of an intellectual double life really marks a triumph of heart over head, of faith's instinct to believe over hesitation born of mental error.

Not that the Evangelical, glad though he is to see such a triumph, will cease to maintain that liberal principles in themselves are arbitrary, un-Christian and harmful. This he ought to do, just as any Christian ought to remonstrate with any fellow-Christian whom he found professing, say, a speculative Arianism, or Pelagianism. Jude's injunction, 'contend earnestly for the faith which was once for all delivered to the saints',[1] applies as directly in the one case as in the other. And the Evangelical will contend with the greatest confidence; for he knows that the faith delivered to the saints, being in the Bible, cannot finally be lost in the Church. The Spirit indwells the Church to witness to Scripture and to what is in Scripture; and while His ministry continues, though mistakes and heresies will no doubt appear in connection with all biblical doctrines, the Church will not finally lapse from any part of the biblical faith. God Himself will maintain His own truth: He will not suffer man to deny it for ever. This doctrine of the authority of God's Word written is part of the biblical faith, plainly taught in Scripture and sealed on the hearts of all God's people by the Holy Ghost; some day, when fashions of thought that

[1] Jude 3, RV.

at present keep many from confessing it have been outmoded, there will be an avowed return to it. Meanwhile, Evangelicals say of it what Gabriel Hebert, as an Anglo-Catholic, says of episcopacy: 'Believing it to be a gift of God and directly related to the Gospel of God, we see in it something which in a re-integrated Christendom must become the possession of all Christians; so that now we who have it hold it in trust for those who have it not.'[1] And they remember the reflection with which Calvin ends the chapter of his *Institutes* from which we quoted: 'Whenever we are troubled at the small number of those who believe, let us counter that by calling to mind that none grasp the mysteries of God save those to whom it is given.'

[1] *Op. cit.*, p. 124.

CHAPTER VI

REASON[1]

How wilt thou say to thy brother, Let me pull out the mote out of thine eye; and, behold, a beam is in thine own eye?

MATTHEW vii. 4

WE saw earlier that some regard the evangelical position as inherently obscurantist. We can imagine what such will say if they have followed our argument thus far. 'This is all very well,' they will tell us, 'but the fact remains that modern scholarship assures us that the Bible does err. That is the conclusion of free scientific enquiry; nothing can alter it, and honest men must face it. You must not wonder if those who will not face it are accused of having wilfully shuttered minds, and sinning against reason and truth. Nor must you wonder that Christians of greater intellectual integrity and realism are at pains to show them the error of their ways. For dishonest thinking, however well-intentioned, can only discredit the cause it serves, and must in the long run boomerang disastrously on those who indulge in it. To plead for the authority of the Bible is a good and necessary work; we do something similar ourselves. But the case cannot be put in your way.' They might add that they do not take seriously the theological scholarship with which evangelical views are defended, for they see it as, of necessity, a pseudo-scholarship, trying to rationalize a position which is both unreasoning and unreasonable. Evangelical scholarship, they say, is blatantly unscientific. The canons of scientific history require one to approach one's sources with an open mind, free from preconceptions about them, and to decide simply on grounds of

[1] An important book for study in connection with this chapter is A. Lecerf, *Introduction to Reformed Dogmatics* (Lutterworth, 1949), especially Part II.

date and character how much or how little confidence one may put in them. But the Evangelical approaches the study of Scripture with his mind made up; he is determined to defend the historicity of all biblical narratives and the truth of all biblical teaching, no matter what mental contortions and special pleading this may involve. Such an unscientific attitude, they tell us, is not merely unscholarly; it is un-Christian. True Christianity is a rational faith; but Evangelicalism counsels blind submission to a book which it is demonstrably irrational to treat as an infallible authority. This is more like murdering reason than redeeming it; it turns the faith of Christ into a bibliolatrous superstition.

We have now reached the point in our argument at which we can address ourselves directly to this criticism. Were it well founded, it would be damning, for the principles to which it appeals are true and right. (They are, indeed, the very principles on which our own case against Liberalism is based, as will appear.) The gospel does in truth proclaim the redemption of reason. Obscurantism is always evil, and wilful error is always sin. All truth is God's truth; facts, as such, are sacred, and nothing is more un-Christian than to run away from them. If Liberals think that this is what Evangelicals do, we cannot expect any sympathy from them for our position, any more than they could expect any sympathy from us for theirs if we thought that they were doing this themselves. This, however, is just what we do think; and we reply to them accordingly. They accuse us of not facing all the facts. We reply that they think this is so only because they themselves do not face all the facts. The boot is on the other foot. They say we fail to meet the claims of reason. We say that they fail to meet the claims of *Christian* reason; and that it is they, rather than we, who weaken the Church's intellectual life, in that they discourage Christians from using their minds in a manner consistent with their faith. We shall now try to make good these contentions, in principle at any rate.

THE PLACE OF REASON IN FAITH

'Reason' means reasoning, as 'faith' means believing and trusting. The first is the mark of men, as distinct from beasts; the second, of Christians, as distinct from unbelievers. As there can be no faith without thinking (for truth must be known before there can be trust), so for the Christian there should be no thinking without faith (for thoughts that do not express faith are sin[1]). The Christian's intellectual vocation is to think about all things in such a way that his life of thought is part of his life of faith and homage to God. Whereas the non-Christian is led by faithless reason, the Christian should be guided by reasoning faith. Broadly speaking, the proper function of reason in relation to faith is threefold:

1. Its first task is to *receive* the teaching of God. Scripture pictures the believer as one who knows himself called to take the attitude of a child, and who is looking to his divine Teacher for instruction.[2] God teaches the Church through the Word, interpreted by the Spirit; accordingly, the Christian seeks the help of the Spirit to enable him to learn what Scripture teaches. His mind is necessarily active in this; biblical interpretation is an exacting mental discipline, and so is systematic theology, the thinking through of the various strands of biblical teaching in the mutual relations in which Scripture sets them. But the Christian does not by his mental labour construct knowledge of God out of his own head, or contribute anything of his own to what God is teaching him; his labour is simply that of receiving and assimilating. He ascribes all the knowledge he gains not to his own keenness of wit, but to the effective instruction of the Holy Spirit. The attitude of mind which he seeks to maintain is that of a pupil who wants to learn as much as his text-book and teacher will tell him, and who therefore attends diligently to them and listens to all that they say. With Charles Simeon, he reminds himself when he approaches Scrip-

[1] Cf. Rom. xiv. 22, 23.

[2] Cf. Pss. xxv. 4 f., cxix. 12 (and nine times more), 71, 73; Mt. xi. 29; Jn. xiv. 26, etc.

ture : 'I know only one thing—that I know nothing.' To say this and mean it is no doubt the hardest task in the world; but this is what he tries to do. He confesses himself blind, stupid and ignorant through sin, and cries to God for enlightenment and instruction.

We have seen already that the biblical revelation terminates in mystery. The lamp of Scripture lights only a limited area of our darkness; beyond that area lie the secrets of God, into which men may not pry. Our knowledge of God, therefore, though true as far as it goes, is nowhere complete or exhaustive. The humble pupil of Scripture will recognize these limits and keep within them. He will not be so self-willed as, on the one hand, to build a speculative theological system which will say more about God than God has said about Himself, or, on the other, to ignore or tone down what Scripture does say because he finds it hard to fit in with the rest of what he knows. His aim is to learn all that God teaches, and give it all its due place in his own thought. And he will never let himself suppose that now he has finished learning and knows everything; instead, he will keep listening to Scripture for further correction and instruction.

The humble pupil of Scripture will trust his text-book and not doubt its claims for itself. Does this mean that he is using his reason uncritically or unscientifically in his study of it? Not at all. Scientific criticism, if it is to be more than an irrelevant testimony to one's own prejudices, must aim to appreciate objects for what they are; its function is to discern their essential nature and to judge them in terms of criteria appropriate to their nature. To find fault with blank verse for not rhyming, for instance, or with a historical novel for adding to the recorded facts, would be very stupid and invalid criticism; it would show failure to grasp the nature of what one was criticizing. Now, we have seen what view of the nature of Scripture Christians should hold—that it is truth from God, profitable for doctrine and instruction. We have seen that this is not a matter of inductive proof, but of divine testimony, received through the witness of the Spirit. Scientific criticism for the Christian, therefore, must mean the effort to understand and appreciate Scripture *as what it is*—God's truth in writing. Such criticism is an exercise of reasoning faith. But to subject Scripture to a scientific critical technique designed to help us tell true from false among fallible human records would be an act of unbelief that was both unscientific and uncritical; for it would be treating Scripture as something other than it is. 'Scientific criticism' would be a complete misnomer for such a procedure. To assume *a priori* that Scripture, like any merely human historical document, is doubtless partly true but also partly false would be a quite unscientific thing to do; for the method of science is to proceed *a posteriori* from the known to the unknown, and Christians know from the teaching of Christ that all Scripture is truth from God. And to form conclusions as to which parts of Scripture are the erroneous ones would be invalid and worthless as criticism, since it would be the result of evaluating Scripture by wholly inappropriate criteria. For Christians to consent to study Scripture on the assumption that it is a fallible human book would not argue intellectual honesty so much as uncritical muddle-headedness; and if they are consistent they will decline to do it. The only biblical criticism which they can consistently regard as valid is that which takes as its starting-point the Bible's account of itself. Much modern criticism within the Christian Church stands self-condemned as unscientific by its arbitrary refusal to take account of what God has told the Church about the nature of Scripture.

Must Bible study conducted on these principles be hidebound and unenterprising? No. It is true that the student will not spend his time in speculative reconstructions of 'real' facts and truths supposed to lie behind, but to vary from, the biblical record; for he will see such enquiries as attempts to answer questions that are based on wrong principles and that should never have been asked. Nor will he develop theories about the origins and authorship of biblical books which go against the Bible's own testimony.[1] Instead, he will set himself to tackle the right

[1] See Appendix II, pp. 182 ff.

questions: namely, what does the Bible actually teach? What does God's written Word mean? What does it say to us? History shows that this, the authentic evangelical approach to Scripture, creates a strong passion for biblical exposition; one has only to think of the expository labours of Luther, Calvin and their successors, whose biblical study could hardly be described as unenterprising! Like them, the modern evangelical student should demand of himself the highest level of scholarly attainment in the fulfilment of his exegetical vocation. In the words of a contemporary spokesman for classical Reformed theology, Professor Auguste Lecerf: 'Every hypothesis which does not deny *a priori* the inspiration of the original text, which does not systematically exclude miracle and prophecy, and presuppose the humanistic ideology of the eighteenth or nineteenth century . . . has a right to the impartial and attentive examination of the Reformed exegete. . . . . We must be prepared to accept loyally the facts as they present themselves and to practise scrupulously the methods of a conscientious critic in the spirit of the faith which has been bestowed upon us and in the liberty indispensable to any science which wishes to be taken seriously.'[1]

2. The second task of Christian reason is to *apply* the teaching of God to life: to bring it into constructive relationship with our other knowledge and interests, and to work out its bearing on the practical problems of daily life and action—moral, social, personal, political, æsthetic, or whatever they may be. This is really an extension of the first task, for the Bible is a book about life and itself instructs us, at any rate in principle, as to the practical bearings of its teaching. Theology must function as the queen of the sciences, showing us how to approach, interpret and use all our knowledge in such a way that the secular order is sanctified to the glory of God. Part of the business of theology is to teach us to see all facts and truths as God's property, of which we are stewards; and so to behave reverently and responsibly in

[1] *Introduction to Reformed Dogmatics*, pp. 313 f.

the world which we acknowledge as His. The need for theology to provide basic principles for interpreting facts becomes greater according to the extent to which the practice of particular intellectual disciplines is affected by the outlook and presuppositions which each student brings to it. There may not be much room for subjectivity in (say) mathematics, but such studies as history, philosophy and the social and psychological sciences are decisively affected by the general assumptions and viewpoint of those who pursue them, and here it is of the first importance that Christians should occupy themselves in thinking out what lines of approach to these studies are consonant with biblical truth.

It is probably true that during the past century Evangelicals have culpably neglected this task of reflecting on the biblical world-view and relating current knowledge to it. This seems to have been due partly to an over-individualistic preoccupation with personal salvation, in which was reflected the typical weakness of the nineteenth-century outlook; partly to the aggressive anti-Christian attitude of much modern science and philosophy, which led many to think that they would be wiser not to take such studies seriously; and partly to the anti-intellectual habit of mind which always threatens warm piety, exalting strong emotion at the expense of clear-headedness and urging that it is more important to feel rightly than to think rightly. (This attitude, of course, was encouraged in the nineteenth century by the work of Schleiermacher.) But in truth this lapse is a tragedy; for it marks a decline from biblical Christianity into a modern form of one of the oldest thorns in the Church's flesh—Manicheism. This is an unfamiliar word today, though it was common enough in the Middle Ages (when bishops and theologians used to use it as a kind of oath for rough-housing obscure opponents, just as some use 'Fundamentalism' today); but the point of view which it denoted is still quite familiar. The Manichean idea was that the material world is evil and worthless. One's dealings with it should therefore be cut down to a bare minimum. True spirituality means living as much out of this world as possible; holiness is to be defined in terms of abstinence from needless traffic with created things. Nothing is gained from the study of anything here below, and the less interest one has in the world around one the better for one's soul.

Such 'spirituality' is in no way Christian; yet it constantly appears in the Christian Church. It would be idle to deny that it is in the air today within evangelical circles, though in fairness it should be said that it is not only they who suffer from this malady. It is evident from their behaviour that some cherish the idea that to take any interest or pleasure in material things is inevitably sinful; that a negative, indifferent attitude to the world around one is a mark of 'keenness', and anything else is 'worldliness'; and, in particular, that constructive thought about the world's contents and problems is no part of a Christian's business. It is to be feared that there are some students—not all of them Evangelicals—who regard their 'academic' and their 'Christian' work as mutually exclusive, and who think it their duty to skimp the former so as to have more time for the latter; there are others who keep their Christian faith and their secular studies locked up in separate compartments in their minds, seeing no need or obligation to bring the two together for their mutual enrichment. Hebert quotes Sir John Wolfenden's much-publicized remark about 'the number of young people who today come from Sixth Forms to Universities with their minds firmly closed, locked, bolted and barred, not just about the Bible and religion in general, but about all sorts of other things as well, philosophy, politics and history among them'.[1] If this was intended as a vignette of the Inter-Varsity Fellowship, it would seem both unfair and untrue; but there is not usually smoke without at least a little fire. All these attitudes that have been mentioned betray the same lack of concern about the world and its problems, and the same unawareness that this lack of concern is in any way un-Christian. The zeal of Christians who have such a negative, Manichean outlook on the world is undoubted (it is, indeed, their very zeal—mis-

[1] *Op. cit.*, p. 140.

guided—that has led them to it); but it is no wonder if they strike others as queer fish, only half alive and oddly under-developed. They give the impression of being not quite human—which is, in fact, the truth about them. That is what Manicheism in the system does for one.

But the Manichean attitude is altogether wrong. God forbids Christians to lose interest in His world. He made man to rule the created order; man is set in it to have dominion over it and to use it for God's glory,[1] and therefore he may, and must, study its contents and its problems. This belongs to his vocation both as a man and as a Christian. The biblical revelation is given us, not merely to show us how to gain heaven, but also to provide us with the principles for glorifying God by creative and imaginative living here and now. We are to use the minds He gave us to apply revealed truth to the whole of life. We are certainly to be detached from the world in the sense that we do not regard it as our true home, nor look to it for our true reward, nor lose our heart to it. That is the point of the biblical warnings against 'worldliness'.[2] Instead of this, we must cultivate the genuine, Christian 'other-worldliness', that of the man who can always say, 'To me to live is Christ, and to die is gain.'[3] But equally certainly we are not to be detached from the world in the sense that we turn our back on it and lose interest in it. God cares about it, and so must we. When Christ enjoins us, as part of the first great commandment, 'Thou shalt love the Lord thy God *with all thy mind*',[4] He is telling us to use our minds not merely to learn biblical doctrine on its own, but to apply that doctrine to the facts of God's world as we know them, so that we may interpret them correctly and make a right and reverent use of our knowledge.

We need, therefore, to be constantly searching Scripture to find what lines of approach it indicates to the problems raised by secular studies—history, natural science, philosophy, psychology and the rest—and how we should view what those studies teach us in the light of

[1] Gn. i. 28.
[2] Cf. 1 Jn. ii. 15 f.; Rom. xii. 2; 2 Tim. iv. 10; Jas. iv. 4.
[3] Phil. i. 21.
[4] Mt. xxii. 37.

God's written truth. Sometimes this will be hard to see; the one may seem to conflict with the other, and there will be tension in our minds. In such cases, our attitude must be determined by the principle that, since the same God is the Author both of nature and of Scripture, true science and a right interpretation of Scripture cannot conflict. We shall, therefore, continue loyal to the evidence both of Scripture and of empirical enquiry, resolved to do justice to all the facts from both sources while we wait for further light as to the right method of relating them together. Meanwhile, we shall look to see whether the appearance of contradiction is not due to mistakes and arbitrary assumptions, both scientific and theological, which a closer scrutiny of the evidence will enable us to correct. It is tempting in such cases to cut the knot and deny the problem, either by discounting one or other set of facts, or by locking them into two separate compartments in our minds and refusing to bring them together; but this, the easy but unrealistic way out, is actually sin (it is always sin to dodge facts), and may well bring its revenge in intellectual upheaval and disillusionment later on. The truth is that the facts of nature yield positive help in many ways for interpreting Scripture statements correctly, and the discipline of wrestling with the problem of relating the two sets of facts, natural and biblical, leads to a greatly enriched understanding of both. Not only does the book of Scripture throw light on the meaning of the book of nature; the book of nature reflects some of that light back on to Scripture, so that we may read its message more clearly. It is through the ferment of thought created by such interaction that theological insight is deepened and the relevance of the gospel more fully grasped.

3. The third task of Christian reason is to *communicate* God's truth to others. The duty of Christian witness involves reasoning, as the descriptions of Paul's missionary activity show.[1] Faith is not created by reasoning, but neither is it created without it. There is more involved in

[1] Cf. Acts xvii. 2, xviii. 4, 19, xxiv. 25.

witness to Christ than throwing pre-arranged clumps of texts at unbelieving heads; the meaning and application of the gospel must be explained to men and women in terms of their actual situation. This requires hard thinking. The biblical revelation was given in terms of Eastern culture, environment and thought-forms, all very different from our modern, industrial, Western world, and it has to be translated into modern terms before modern men can fully grasp its relevance. Biblical terms and images (sin, justification, sacrifice, covenant, holiness, priest, blood, spirit, for instance) are not self-explanatory; it is therefore our task as witnesses for Christ to seek out ways and means of making their meaning clear.

Not that we may alter or revise the gospel in order to make it more palatable to the modern mind. That would be treachery to Christ. Our business is to present the Christian faith clothed in modern terms, not to propagate modern thought clothed in Christian terms. Our business is to interpret and criticize modern thought by the gospel, not *vice versa*. Confusion here is fatal. The formula 'of course, nowadays we don't believe . . .' should find no place in modern re-statements of the gospel; its appearance (a common thing, unfortunately) is usually a sign that what is being stated is, to that extent, not the gospel, but a denial of the gospel; and such statements come under Paul's curse, to which we referred before.[1] Nor, again, may we present the faith as a philosophy, to be accepted (if at all) on grounds of rational demonstration; we must always declare it as revealed truth, divinely mysterious and transcending reason's power to verify, to be received humbly on the authority of God. Faith involves the renunciation of intellectual self-sufficiency; we must always proclaim the gospel in a way that makes this clear. That was the point of Paul's protest against the Corinthian desire to arrange a marriage between the gospel of Christ crucified and the 'wisdom of words' of the Greek tradition. The gospel, he insisted, makes foolish the wisdom of this world—that is, it shows the bankruptcy of proud, self-sufficient reason and condemns it; and his

[1] Gal. i. 8, 9.

own method of preaching the gospel was deliberately designed to wean aspiring philosophers from reliance on their reason and shut them up to humble, self-distrustful dependence on God's Word and Spirit for light and understanding. 'My speech and my preaching were not in persuasive words of wisdom, but in demonstration of the Spirit and of power; that your faith should not stand in the wisdom of men, but in the power of God.'[1]

J. R. W. Stott well sums up the position: 'In evangelism, then, we shall need to recognize that the men to whom we preach have minds. We shall not ask them to stifle their minds, but to open them, and in particular to open them to receive a divine illumination in order to understand the divine revelation. We shall not seek to murder their intellect (since it was given to them by God), but neither shall we flatter it (since it is finite and fallen). We shall endeavour to reason with them, but only from revelation, the while admitting our need and theirs for the enlightenment of the Holy Spirit.'[2]

THE CONFLICT BETWEEN REASON AND FAITH

Such, in outline, are the biblical principles governing the Christian use of reason. Why are those who try, however inadequately, to be loyal to these principles told that they are incorrigible obscurantists, and that their minds are not free?

Let us put the matter in its broader setting. What confronts us in this complaint of obscurantism is one more outbreak of a conflict that has been in progress within the Christian Church since it was founded. It is sometimes called (not very happily) the conflict between faith and reason. It always takes essentially the same form. Whereas the logic of faith requires us, as we saw, to challenge and correct secular opinion by the light of revealed truth, the self-styled champions of reason always desire to bring the biblical faith into line with secular ideas. A few examples may be given. In the second century, Gnosticism aspired to remodel the doctrine of salvation in the

[1] 1 Cor. ii. 4, 5, RV; see the whole passage, i. 17–ii. 16.
[2] *Fundamentalism and Evangelism*, p. 25.

light of an Oriental dualism which taught that matter, as such, was evil; salvation, therefore, it was held, should be conceived as deliverance from the body and the material world. In the fourth century, Arianism aspired to remodel the Church's Christology by the light of Greek philosophical ideas about God, which made it impossible to think of Jesus Christ as divine. In the eighteenth century, the Deists wished to remodel the doctrine of providence in the light of the then-popular view of the universe as a self-contained machine, and to make men think of God as an absentee landlord, who had left His world to run itself. The nineteenth-century Liberals tried to remodel the doctrines of human nature and grace in the light of the theory of evolution, maintaining that sin was just a transitional stage in the steady march of mankind, under Christ's leadership, towards inevitable perfection. And their twentieth-century children (the present-day critics of Evangelicalism), though they have generally returned to a more biblical view of man and his redemption, are anxious today to remodel the doctrine of revelation in the light of the rationalistic biblical criticism which they have inherited. All attempts of this sort to refurbish faith by reason rest on the same assumption, implicit if not explicit—namely, that the human mind, working by its own light, is the final arbiter of truth, even in the things of God; or, putting it another way, that some form of the subjectivist doctrine of authority is true. And when the champions of reason complain (as they regularly do) that Christians who reject their views keep reason from its rights and deny it freedom, all they are really doing is calling attention to the fact that the latter do not accept their unscriptural views about authority.

It is not, perhaps, surprising to find Christians constantly, often unconsciously, lapsing into subjectivist assumptions. For when men become Christians they do not cease to be sinners; and the attitude of mind which the subjectivist position expresses—that epitomized by Protagoras, five centuries before Christ, in the famous phrase 'man is the measure of all things'—is one which, Scripture tells us, is natural to sinful men. It was precisely because man welcomed the prospect of becoming the measure and judge of all things that sin first entered the world. 'When you eat . . . your eyes will be opened, and you will be like God, knowing good and evil,' affirmed the serpent.[1] It was as though he said: 'You will not need to depend any more on what God chooses to tell you; you will be able to work out for yourselves what is good and bad, and be master of your own judgment, on the basis of your own experience; you will have a mind of your own for the first time.' 'So when the woman saw that . . . the tree was to be desired to make one wise, she took of its fruit and ate,' and Adam with her. Man accepted the invitation to pursue wisdom by constructing a private interpretation of life out of the resources of his own independent judgment. He sought intellectual self-sufficiency, ability to solve all life's problems without reference to the word of God. He turned his back on the way of acquiring wisdom by making God's statements the criterion for his judgment; indeed, he accepted the serpent's assurance that wisdom could not be had that way at all. He had the audacity to query God's word. Pride, and more particularly intellectual pride, was thus the root of his sin.

And this same outlook has been natural to man ever since. Sinners are no more ready to acknowledge God in their thinking, by allowing His utterances authority over their judgment, than they are to acknowledge God in their actions, by allowing His utterances authority over their behaviour. Sin has its root in the mind, and this attitude of mind is its very essence. And when men become Christians, they are still prone in their pride to lapse into the assumption that there is no rationality or wisdom in merely taking their Creator's word; they are still apt to demand instead that their reason be permitted to make its own independent assessment of what He says and to have the last word in deciding whether it is credible or not. This is as real and gross a moral lapse as any, though it is not always seen as such; and the temptation to it is strong and insidious. And once one succumbs, and relapses to any degree into this sinful habit of mind, one is instantly drawn

[1] Gn. iii. 5, RSV.

to the conclusion that Christians who continue to base their thinking on an unquestioning belief of what God has said are fettering reason and stifling free thought. No doubt the serpent would have told Eve as much, had she asked him.

But it is not so. The true antithesis here, as we have seen, is not between faith and reason (as if believing and thinking were mutually exclusive), but between a faithful and a faithless use of reason. The question is not whether we should think, but how we should think; whether or not our thinking should be controlled by our faith. The real difference between Evangelicals and those who call them obscurantists lies in the realm of method. We disagree as to the principles that should guide the Christian judgment. Our critics say that the way in which we deal with the Bible is fundamentally dishonest. We reply that they think so only because the way in which they deal with the Bible is fundamentally un-Christian. They hold that what needs revision is our doctrine of biblical authority; but it seems that what really needs revision is their method of biblical scholarship. Instead of subjecting their own judgment wholly to Scripture, they subject Scripture in part to their own judgment. They treat the question of the truth and authority of Scripture, which God has closed, as if it were still open; they assume the right and competence of the Christian student to decide for himself how much of the Bible's teaching should be received as authoritative. They accept what they do accept, not simply because it is Scripture, but because it satisfies some further criteria of credibility which they have set up; so that even when they believe the right thing, in so far as they are consistent subjectivists they do so for the wrong reason. Their whole approach to the Bible is fundamentally unbiblical.

We see now how fallacious it is for them to think that the question as to whether the Bible is inerrant or not can be settled by appeal to the work of modern scholars and 'the assured results of biblical criticism'. Whether or not one is prepared to postulate that the Bible may contain falsehoods purporting to be truths is a matter of presupposition and method. Liberals will tell us that they hold their views about Scripture 'on critical grounds', as if that phrase explains everything. In fact, it explains nothing. What are these 'critical grounds'? On examination, they are found to derive from un-biblical principles of judgment for interpreting biblical evidence. These 'assured results of modern criticism' are simply popular hypotheses built on the inadmissible assumption that there may be untrue statements in Scripture.

The general question which Christian students must face before ever they tackle specific critical issues is this: should the principles governing our study of Scripture be drawn from Scripture itself, or not? It is not a hard question to answer. Christian believers, who acknowledge the authority of Christ as a Teacher in other matters, ought equally to acknowledge it in their approach to the Bible; they should receive Scripture as He did, accepting its claim to be divinely inspired and true and studying it as such. Those who pooh-pooh such an approach as obscurantist, unscientific and intellectually dishonest, should remember that they hereby stigmatize Jesus Christ, who taught His disciples this approach and thereby excluded any other.

We would not be misunderstood. We have nothing to say in defence of the real obscurantism which would ignore altogether the questions raised by modern critical enquiry. We deplore the idea that Evangelicals ought to have, or look for, ready-made 'party-line' answers to all these problems. On many questions of biblical history and exposition there is room for real and legitimate difference of opinion, and no doubt always will be. All that we insist on is that no critical discussion is sound or legitimate that is not based on the Bible's own view of itself. We entirely agree with Hebert that in Bible study 'we are required to be at once humble and docile, and alert and critical. We must be critical; an entirely uncritical person would be entirely gullible, foolish and superstitious. . . . The ideal biblical student would have to be as sharply and even daringly critical as is humanly possible, and at the same time deeply sensitive to the things of the spirit, and so far as his will goes entirely obedient to God's will.'[1] Our whole complaint against the modern critical movement is that its exponents have not been alert and critical enough; they have failed to criticize the assumptions which their critical method enshrines. It is for sharp and even daring criticism at this point that we now plead. Evangelicals dissent from 'critical orthodoxy' not because they are wilfully ignorant of its conclusions, but because they are acutely conscious of the illegitimacy of its method. They seek to be obedient to God's will by reforming biblical criticism according to His Word; they advocate a Christian critique of critical method; for they are sure that criticism should be of a piece with faith, not wedded to axioms which represent a lapse into unbelief.

Hebert tells us that the older Liberalism is now dead, and has been replaced by the 'Biblical Theology' movement. 'The characteristic of this Biblical Theology is that it is at once deeply orthodox in faith, and thoroughly critical—more critical than the Liberal critics, since it is also critical of the critics themselves.' Those associated with this movement, he tells us, 'endeavour to see the Bible "from within"; not to impose on it standards of judgment derived from any modern belief in "progress", but to sit at their feet (its authors') and learn from them what they are seeking to express.'[2] We welcome this statement of aims, to which we would ourselves wholeheartedly subscribe; we can only hope that its adherents will soon act upon it in regard to the doctrine of Scripture. It is hard to believe that they take their professed aims seriously when they charge Evangelicals with obscurantism for believing the 'Jewish' doctrine of Scripture, the only one that the Bible knows, and when Dr. Hebert himself writes a complete book on 'Fundamentalism' without discussing at all the avowed biblicism of our Lord and His apostles, nor the biblical concepts of Scripture and of its authority. The exponents of 'Biblical Theology' have yet to convince Evangelicals that they are completely sincere in saying that they desire to see the Bible 'from within', and to break with the arbitrary subjectivism of the older

[1] *Op. cit.*, p. 11. [2] *Op. cit.*, pp. 22 f.

Liberals. If they wish to gain the confidence of Evangelicals, they must show an attitude to the Bible more earnestly biblical than that which they adopt at present.

THE FREEDOM OF REASON SECURED BY FAITH

We end by replying directly to the criticism with which this chapter began. Do evangelical principles inhibit the freedom of reason? On the contrary, they establish it. Freedom is no merely negative conception; anarchy is not freedom, either on the moral or on the intellectual level. True freedom is something positive: to possess it is to fulfil one's human destiny. Such freedom is found only in subjection to God and His truth; and the more subject, the more free—this is the biblical paradox of Christian liberty. Man becomes free only in bondservice to Jesus Christ; otherwise, he is captive to sin. Man's mind becomes free only when its thoughts are brought into captivity to Christ and His Word; till then, it is at the mercy of sinful prejudice and dishonest mental habits within, and of popular opinion, organized propaganda and unquestioned commonplaces without. Tossed about by every wind of intellectual fashion and carried to and fro by cross-currents of reaction, man without God is not free for truth; he is for ever mastered by the things he takes for granted, the victim of a hopeless and everlasting relativism. Only as his thoughts are searched, challenged and corrected by God through His Word may man hope to rise to a way of looking at things which, instead of reflecting merely passing phases of human thought, reflects God's eternal truth. This is the only road to intellectual freedom, and its sole safeguard is the principle of absolute subjection to Scripture. If, as our critics say, Evangelicals at present are not entering into this heritage, that does not mean that it is not theirs to enter into. The truth is that, in principle, it is theirs and no one else's; for they alone treat the idea of biblical authority seriously enough to secure and preserve this freedom. If anyone in the present debate lacks intellectual freedom, it is rather those whose minds are governed by the tyrannical modern axiom that what is newest must be truest, what is old must be out-of-date, and change is always progress; those who feel they must deny what Christ affirmed about Scripture rather than break with nineteenth-century ideas of what assumptions are 'scientific' and what are not; those in the grip of a theological neurosis that makes them regard rationalistic principles of biblical criticism as an inviolable sacred cow. Because they submit to Scripture only in part, their minds are not wholly free for truth; by maintaining a fancied freedom (non-subjection to God's Word), they forfeit the possibility of real freedom; nor can they gain the second till they renounce the first. They may be right in saying that modern Evangelicals are intellectually hidebound; but it is the pot that is calling the kettle black. And the kettle can be cleaned—please God, it will be, as Evangelicalism recovers its native intellectual vigour in our own day—but the pot will have to be discarded and replaced.

Are evangelical principles obscurantist? No. The truth is that Evangelicals face facts which the exponents of 'critical orthodoxy' overlook: namely, that the Bible teaches a positive doctrine of its origin and nature, which Christ incorporated in His own teaching. The position that is really obscurantist is that of those who refuse to face these facts, and will not consider that to reject Christ's teaching about the Bible is as sinful and faithless as to reject His teaching on anything else. If the adjective 'heretical' has any place in this debate, it is surely here that it ought to be applied.

'I beseech you in the bowels of Christ, think it possible you may be mistaken,' wrote Oliver Cromwell on a famous occasion to the General Assembly of the Scottish Church. We address a similar plea to some in high places in British churches today. We ask them to think it possible they may be mistaken in attributing intellectual dishonesty to those who cannot stomach the idea that God's witness to His Word is untrue, and who think it likelier that man has erred than that God has lied. We would ask them to think it possible they may be mistaken in supposing that only minds which lapse into unbiblical ways of thought are open and free, whereas minds which do not are fettered and closed. We would ask them to think it possible they may be mistaken when they detect in evangelical evangelism a summons to stifle the mind. We do indeed summon sinners to bow before the authority of the written Word of God; but this is a call, not to stop thinking, but to stop thinking sinfully, and to start bringing one's thoughts into captivity to Christ. Repentance means 'change of mind'; and the call to submit to biblical authority is part of the preaching of repentance—a summons to intellectual prodigals to return to the Father's house and start thinking normally again, using their minds not as tools of pride, but in humility and obedience, as children of a heavenly Father should do.

CHAPTER VII

LIBERALISM

And he answered, I have not troubled Israel; but thou, and thy father's house, in that ye have forsaken the commandments of the Lord.

I KINGS xviii. 18

Can the Ethiopian change his skin, or the leopard his spots?

JEREMIAH xiii. 23

WE have on occasion referred to our critics as Liberals. This requires justification, for most of them would not call themselves by this name, and our use of it might therefore seem as invidious as their use of 'Fundamentalist' seemed to be. But we needed a generic term that would cover all those who are wedded to the methods of nineteenth-century biblical criticism, and none seemed available save that to which its first advocates laid claim. Their present-day disciples profess to occupy a position so different from that of the early Liberals that it is unfair to lump them together. We continue to do so, however, because we doubt whether this claim is valid; the differences seem to be superficial, while the subjectivist principle which underlay original Liberalism remains unchanged. Our reasons for thinking so will appear in the following pages, the aim of which is to consider the adequacy of the standpoint from which the current polemic against 'Fundamentalism' has been launched.

OLD LIBERALISM

We shall understand our critics' position best by reviewing its historical origins.

The ideals of the nineteenth-century liberal movement found expression in a demand for justice to be done to the human characteristics of the Bible. It was pointed out that each book has its own cultural and historical background, and that these factors must not be neglected in interpreting it. It was affirmed that the primarily dogmatic interest of earlier expositors had led them to confine their attention to the doctrinal bearing of their texts while neglecting to study them in their historical setting; with the result that often they failed to see their real significance, and read into them meanings which, though verbally possible, were historically indefensible. Thus the dogmatic use of texts was itself often incorrect. More accurate historical exegesis, it was said, was urgently needed to correct this weakness. The way to a fuller grasp of the abiding divine truth of the Bible was to study the human features of its various books more intensively.

There was some truth in these strictures on earlier expositors, though, as anyone who has studied the Reformers and seventeenth-century Protestant exegetes knows, not nearly so much as is sometimes suggested. (An often-repeated shibboleth of 'critical orthodoxy' is that one century of critical study has taught the Church more about the Bible than was learned in all the previous eighteen; but this absurd claim can only be accounted for as a twentieth-century hangover of nineteenth-century bumptiousness.) There is no dispute, however, that Scripture must be interpreted historically. Protestants never doubted it; and it was no fault of Liberalism to insist upon it.

Unfortunately, however, the historical researches of the early Liberals were marred by the intrusion of unbiblical assumptions drawn from secular thought. A mixture of motives can be detected in their work which bears a sad witness to human frailty. On the one hand, they were determined that their studies should be genuinely scientific, not governed by dogmatic theological bias of a kind that would make them bad history. That was admirable. They wished to recommend Christianity to the secularized 'modern mind' of their day, and so to enrich apologetics as well as theology. That was admirable, too. But they were too anxious to be up-to-date and bowed to current fashions of thought quite uncritically. As a result, they did their work under the influence of a dogmatic philosophical bias which made it both bad history and bad Christianity.

In the first place, they accepted the viewpoint of the Romantic philosophy of religion set out by Schleiermacher—namely that the real subject-matter of theology is not divinely revealed truths, but human religious experience. On this view, the proper study of theologians, after all, is man. The Bible is a record of human action and reflection within which is embedded an experience of God, and our task is to dig that experience out. Scripture must be viewed, not as a divinely given record of a divinely given revelation, but as a by-product of the religious experience of the Hebrews; a record not so much of what God has said and done as of what some men thought He had said and done. The Bible is thus a memorial of the discovery of God by a nation with a flair for religion—that, and no more. The adoption of this approach was represented as a great advance. What it actually meant was that the pendulum had swung from the traditional habit of regarding Scripture only, or at least chiefly, as a divine book containing doctrinal truths to a new habit of regarding it only as a human book, a record of religious experiences. Each approach, as we have seen, corresponds to one aspect of the truth, for the Bible is both fully human and fully divine. But if one factor must be stressed at the expense of the other, far less is lost by treating the Scriptures simply as the written oracles of God than simply as a collection of Jewish ideas about God. For we have no reason to regard merely human words as inerrant and authoritative; what will be authoritative for us, if we take the liberal view, is our own judgment as to how far they may be trusted and how far not. Thus we land, willy-nilly, in subjectivism; which, as we saw, is a radical perversion of Christianity.

Then, in the second place, the early Liberals relied on the idea of evolution as the key to interpreting the religious process out of which the Bible came. This was understandable, for at that time leaders of thought were inclined to treat evolution as the master-key which unlocks the meaning of every process of change, biological, moral, social and cultural, as well as religious. To the nineteenth-century mind, 'scientific' study meant study done on an evolutionary hypothesis, and a 'scientific' explanation of facts was one which showed, in terms of such a hypothesis, how the higher had developed out of something lower in the scale of life. But this use of evolutionary principles to explain biblical religion was disastrous. For the Bible is quite clear that the history of Israel's faith was not an evolutionary process, developing from within; it presents that history rather as an expanding series of divine revelations of mercy given against a background of recurring apostasy and degeneration. In so far as the Bible records religious processes originating from within man, they are processes of decline—degeneration from the fall to the flood, idolatry in Canaan after the conquest, deepening apostasy after the division of the kingdom, spiritual backsliding after the return from exile, Israel's hardening of heart in Christ's day, and the wholesale corruption of mankind which Paul describes in Romans i. The Liberals, however, paid no attention to this. In defiance of the biblical evidence, they forced the religious history of Israel into an evolutionary mould which made the prophets, not Moses, the first expositors of ethical monotheism. Scripture presents the prophets as restoring, expounding and augmenting the faith and law revealed through Moses; but this was dismissed as an idealized picture without foundation in fact. Moreover, the Liberals insisted on viewing the development of Israel's religion as a steady process of outgrowing primitive ideas, with Christianity as the final refinement. This made necessary a cavalier treatment of the New Testament. The Liberals were sure that such 'primitive' notions as the wrath of God, propitiatory sacrifice and supernatural redemption had no place in the religion of Jesus. True (they said), these ideas crept out from the dark corners of retrograde Judaism and Hellenistic cults into the minds of the early Christians, so that we find them in the New Testament; but they have no business there. Harnack, the coryphæus of Liberalism at the turn of the century, reduced essential Christianity to three things: the universal Fatherhood of God, the infinite worth of the human soul, and the law of love to one's fellow-men.[1] The background of this reconstruction, with its complete elimination of redemptive acts of God, was a dogma which all evolutionary theories presuppose—the unbroken uniformity of nature. Liberal minds were hostile to any idea of supernatural redemptive intrusions into this world-order, and worked hard to eliminate them from their faith; with what result we saw earlier.[2]

What judgment should we pass on the liberal experiment? In an essay entitled 'The Failure of Liberalism to interpret the Bible as the Word of God', Professor T. W. Manson gives a just verdict: 'The attempt of Liberalism to deal with the history of biblical religion was vitiated by its dogmatic presuppositions. Having taken up its axioms, which were at variance with the fundamental ideas of the Bible, there was no way of carrying the business through which did not involve picking and choosing among the biblical material on a scale and with an arbitrariness quite impossible to justify. . . . All was done with the very best intentions, in the firm belief that Liberalism was on the side of progress, and that the purification and strengthening of the Christian religion was now in full swing. The truth, now coming clearly to light, is that Christianity was being gently and gradually transformed into humanism. . . .'[3] Christianity, in fact, was ceasing to be Christianity. This was what Warfield and Machen saw so clearly, as we noted above.[4] What, then, needs to be done? Should we give up the historical study of Scripture? Indeed no. Professor Manson tells us what we must do. 'We must retrace our steps to the point where Liberalism went off the track; and, having reached that point, we must go forward not backward.'[5]

[1] See *What is Christianity?* (2nd ed., 1901).

[2] Pp. 25 ff. above.

[3] *The Interpretation of the Bible*, ed. C. W. Dugmore (S.P.C.K., 1944), pp. 102 f.

[4] Pp. 25, 27 above.

[5] *Op. cit.*, p. 101.

NEW LIBERALISM

But here someone will interject: 'Exactly; and the thing has now been done. Why do you spend so much time belabouring old-fashioned Liberalism? You are flogging a dead horse. And if you think that those who disagree with you hold such views, you are very much mistaken.' For proof of this, he will quote Dr. Hebert's assertion that old Liberalism has now been abandoned in favour of 'Biblical Theology', the new approach which seeks to read the Bible 'from within'.[1] 'Now,' he will say, 'can you not see that this is precisely the approach to the Bible which you yourself advocate? This, and nothing else, is the modern Protestant programme for Bible study. The one aim of your critics is to be biblical. By what right, then, do you continue to call them "Liberals", and treat them as if they were heretics?'

To this we would make a double reply.

In the first place, we would suggest that it shows a somewhat naïve and unrealistic optimism to say that old-fashioned Liberalism is dead. It may be dead at the top, among leading theologians (though even this, one suspects, is an over-statement); but those who study Scripture in schools and training colleges (for instance) know that it is not yet dead there. That some of those who are most outspoken against 'Fundamentalism' are Liberals of the old type seems to be simple matter of fact.

In the second place, we would say this:

We are indeed aware of the transformation that has taken place in liberal circles. It is reflected by the fact that, whereas fifty years ago the chief charge against Evangelicalism was that it was too exclusively biblical, today the cry is that it is 'not biblical enough'.[2] Liberalism is returning to the old paths. Most modern theologians have given up the evolutionary philosophy of the last century and the idea that theology is a mere verbal index of religious experience; they are again ready to affirm the unique deity of Christ and the finality of the Christian revelation; the

[1] Hebert, *op. cit.*, pp. 22 f.; quoted above, p. 142.
[2] So P. Lee-Woolf, *art. cit.*, p. 36.

supernaturalism of the historic creeds no longer embarrasses them; and they acknowledge the reality of divine action in the world in miracles, in the work of Christ, in the conversion of Christians and in the government of history. Holes are being steadily knocked into 'critical orthodoxy' as biblical scholars move back to more conservative views; Moses and the patriarchs have been largely rehabilitated; the antiquity of the Mosaic law is now generally recognized; the substantial historicity of the Gospels and correspondence between Christ's Christianity and apostolic teaching are no longer in question. We are glad to note how much stress is laid today on the unity of the Bible as a record of redemption. We gratefully acknowledge that 'Biblical Theology' has already produced much valuable raw material for the theologian, just as, for all its faults, old Liberalism did for the biblical historian. We welcome too the announced programme of the 'Biblical Theology' movement. If its sponsors carried it through, there would indeed be no controversy between Liberals and Evangelicals, for the former would be found on the evangelical side. Unfortunately, however, this does not happen; and it is not hard to see why.

The truth is, as we have already hinted, that the exponents of 'Biblical Theology' are caught in a dilemma. They can hardly be unaware that, if they were consistent in reading the Bible 'from within' and receiving what its authors were concerned to teach, they would be led to the doctrine of Scripture which we have expounded; for that doctrine is integral to the biblical faith. But they are unready to face this; for they are determined to maintain that the only right route into the Bible is that marked out by the use of old Liberalism's critical method—the method which assumes the propriety of treating the Bible as something other than 'Scripture' in the biblical sense of that word. We know why this is : it is because they rightly desire that their Bible study should be scientific and critical. But, as we have argued already, the rationalistic method of nineteenth-century criticism is both unscientific and uncritical, for it rests on an uncriticized false assumption about the nature of the Bible. Again, we know that 'Biblical Theologians' are concerned lest the real gains of the past century's Bible study—which we would not for a moment deny—should be lost in an obscurantist reaction. But they are quite mistaken in supposing that the true results of sound exegesis can be conserved only by clinging to the false method that vitiates so much so-called 'critical' study. What is needed is that the false method be replaced by a true one, and that the true insights which have come through the great archæological and linguistic advances of the past century be synthesized on right principles. This, however, 'Biblical Theologians' seem unable to see; they think themselves still bound to use critical methods which are in fact unbiblical. Hence they regularly revert to the subjectivist principle of authority for the purposes of biblical criticism; they still propose to themselves the question whether particular biblical statements are true or false, and still on occasion allow themselves to conclude 'on critical grounds' that Scripture is in error. And they maintain that this discipline is a necessary preliminary to believing theological study: in other words, that we must study the Bible as unbelievers before we are entitled to study it, or what is left of it, in a way consistent with faith. This position is still, in principle, Liberalism; and the only significant difference between the new Liberalism and the old seems to be that the former lays more stress than did the latter on the importance of *believing* the more or less mangled Bible that comes out of the critical mincing-machine.

What the 'Biblical Theology' movement has done is to throw into relief the inner contradiction of Liberalism. That contradiction was always there, for Liberalism is subjectivism trying to be Christianity, and, as we saw, subjectivism in any form is incompatible with Christianity. The Christian position is that we know God and His truth only by receiving the testimony which He has borne to Himself, and any attempt to qualify or re-fashion the contents of this testimony actually falsifies it. To defer to God's Word is an act of faith; any querying and editing of it on our own initiative is an exhibition of unbelief. The liberal attempt to produce a subjectivist Christianity was an attempt to yoke the outlook of faith to methods and techniques consistent only with unbelief, and it could not, in the nature of the case, lead to anything but an unstable, oscillating compromise. Old Liberalism sought both to amend the biblical record of facts by 'scientific' historical criticism and to re-interpret those facts in their reconstructed state, in terms of the 'scientific outlook'. We saw Machen pointing out that, if this were consistently done, supernatural Christianity would perish altogether. But in fact the evolutionary critique was carried only a certain distance. The older Liberals were anxious to be up-to-date nineteenth-century men, and found the Christian biblical tradition somewhat embarrassing; but their own Christian instincts proved too strong for them, and they did not as a body go all the way they had marked out for themselves. Now the pendulum has swung back. The new Liberals are anxious to be biblical in their beliefs, and condemn old Liberalism as heretical;[1] but they are held back from a consistently biblical outlook by the legacy of rationalistic criticism which they have inherited. 'We must at all costs and in all matters be biblical,' says the 'Biblical Theology' movement in effect, 'but we must on no account abandon the unbiblical methods of biblical criticism which the heretical Liberals of the last century worked out.' The self-contradictory character of liberal Christianity has never become more evident than here. But it is not possible in fact to eat one's cake and have it.

The inner ambiguity of 'Bible Theology' may be shown in this way. The slogan of the movement is that faith must be based on historical enquiry. In the words of Hoskyns, which Hebert quotes approvingly: 'The Christian religion is not merely open to historical investigation, but demands it, and its piety depends upon it.'[2] Now, we ask, what conception of historical enquiry is in view here? Is it the enquiry of those who, accepting in advance that what Scripture says is true, desire simply to learn its meaning? Or is it the enquiry of those who, without any such presupposition, are trying to estimate the credibility of the biblical record and reconstruct what

[1] So Hebert, *op cit.*, pp. 24, 78.

[2] *Op. cit.*, p. 23.

actually happened? If the former is intended, then this study of biblical history is itself an activity and expression of faith, and faith depends on it only in the secondary sense that historical exegesis is needed to discover what Scripture means. And in this sense the slogan is true. But the spokesmen of this movement insist that they do not mean it in this sense at all. To study Scripture with one's mind made up in advance as to its truth is to them 'unscientific', 'not honest', and in no way commendable. What they have in mind, they tell us, is the latter alternative, historical enquiry into the truth of Scripture which is 'free' and 'unbiased' (i.e., divorced from faith in Scripture).

Well, we reply, if that is the position of 'Biblical Theology', certain things clearly follow. First, it is plain that the ordinary layman, not being a trained historian, will have to take the contents of his faith second-hand from the expert. The historian, therefore, is the real mediator between God and men. And thus 'Biblical Theology' breeds a new authoritarianism. It allows historians to live by the subjectivist doctrine of authority, using their trained judgment in critical scrutiny of Scripture; but it compels the rest of us to take the traditionalist position and bow to the pronouncements of the Church's historical experts. Moreover, we ask, what are we to do when we find the experts disagreed?—as we usually do, for the unanimous consent of the historians is as elusive as the unanimous consent of the Fathers. How are we to choose between historian and historian? Why should we opt for (say) Hoskyns and Hebert rather than (say) Harnack or Bultmann? Under pressure from these questions, we find the 'Biblical Theologians' changing their ground. Oh, we are told, the historians whom we should follow are those who are themselves believers, and whose work is based on catholic Christian presuppositions. But this is to go back to the first position, which a moment ago was rejected! The truth is that 'Biblical Theology' wants to have it both ways. It wants to tell us, on the one hand, that critical Bible study must be 'scientific' and 'free'—free, that is, from biblical assumptions; and, on the other hand, that the biblical critics who may be trusted are those whose work is controlled by such assumptions. It wants to be able to commend itself to the world as scientific, because it holds to the unorthodox views of nineteenth-century critics, and to the Church as Christian, because it deals with 'the biblical point of view'. It seeks a critical method that is both scientific and believing; but what it actually does is to evolve one that succeeds in being neither, but oscillates arbitrarily between two incompatible centres of reference.

This unresolved contradiction runs right through Hebert's *Fundamentalism and the Church of God*. F. D. Kidner has called attention to it. 'Hebert . . . wishes to treat faith as sovereign. But the title turns out to be only honorific. . . . We find the author, on the one hand, insisting that this school of thought conducts its biblical criticism from "deeply orthodox" presuppositions—which can only mean that conviction has preceded criticism. . . . On the other hand, he lays it down that "there can be no honest inquiry if the conclusions are determined before it starts"—which in turn can only mean that criticism must precede conviction. . . . He is left with two masters to serve; and he ends, for all his protestations, by making faith wait on criticism.'[1] Hebert's root error here is that he habitually thinks of scientific historical criticism as something which is not a function of faith, but which functions independently of faith and, indeed, in a way incompatible with it. He draws a distinction between the interpretation of historical facts (in which, as he recognizes, faith is the controlling factor) and the determination of these facts, 'the investigation of the factual course of events', and maintains that in the latter sphere (in which history is most properly 'scientific') 'a decision must be reached solely on the basis of the evidence'. At this stage, Christian beliefs must be left out of account : 'no external presupposition, such as a doctrine of Inerrancy or the articles of the Christian Creed, can influence the estimate of the evidence.' Why not? Because 'the appeal of the Christian

[1] Review in *Inter-Varsity*, Autumn 1957, p. 17.

Faith is to the facts'.[1] But if God has told us, among other things, that what Scripture says is true, is that not a fact, and a relevant fact? Do articles of faith lack status as facts? In any case, we cannot estimate the evidence for the facts of faith without external presuppositions of the sort that Hebert would exclude. For the evidence is in each case Scripture statements; and our evaluation of Scripture statements will be affected by whether we believe such statements to be inerrant or not; and the one attitude is an 'external presupposition' as much as the other. Again, the evidence concerns alleged supernatural interventions —the exodus, the incarnation, the miracles, the resurrection—and our evaluation of it will necessarily depend on our prior judgment as to the possibility of such things.

Hebert's distinction, then, will not hold. It is an illusion to suppose that anyone's study of the facts of faith can ever be neutral. If 'scientific' study of them means study with no presuppositions at all, there has never been such a thing in this world. Presuppositions come in the moment we start evaluating our data. Our verdict on the biblical evidence will itself be an interpretation of that evidence, and our interpretation will either express faith, or not; and if not faith, then unbelief in one form or another. Hebert's concern is to secure for the Christian study of biblical history a genuinely 'scientific' character; but he misconceives the way to do this, because he cannot rid himself of the idea—the incubus of the whole 'Biblical Theology' movement—that historical enquiry is only 'scientific' when it is divorced from Christian presuppositions. But the right way to meet this concern is to make it clear that 'scientific', 'objective' study of anything is simply study of it in terms of itself, and that Scripture is studied 'scientifically' and 'objectively' when—and only when—it is studied in full recognition of its character as Scripture, the infallible Word of God.

Our hope for the 'Biblical Theology' movement is that it will some day take its own announced programme seriously enough to embrace the biblical principle of biblical authority, and to submit its unbiblical notions of 'scientific

[1] *Op. cit.*, p. 74.

history' and 'biblical criticism' to the judgment of God's written Word. Meanwhile, it does not seem unfair to speak of it as a kind of Liberalism; for, though it has rejected the evolutionary outlook of old Liberalism, it has not abandoned the liberal conception of the nature of scientific Bible study. Its equilibrium, therefore, cannot but be unstable, for two incompatible approaches to Christianity are striving to dominate its thinking: that of consistent faith, and that of consistent unbelief. As a result, every reconstruction of Christian truth which this school produces is bound to seem—and really to be—inconsistent and arbitrary, sustained in being by the will of the scholar rather than by the logic of his principles. Always we shall be left asking: if he really approached the Bible with Christian presuppositions, why does he not believe more? and if he really approached it without them, why does he not believe less? No doubt he will on occasion, with Hebert, profess to have done both; but in fact he will have done neither consistently. What he will have done is to follow 'the biblical point of view' just so far as (on 'critical grounds') he thought he would; but no further. Accordingly, his claim to have parted company with Liberalism must be disallowed. He is, at bottom, a subjectivist still.

We watch, then, to see which way the cat will jump: whether 'Biblical Theology' will move on to an explicit Evangelicalism, or fall back into a full-blown subjectivism; whether, that is, the scepticism of its Bible study will be corrected by the biblical faith which it professes, or whether that profession itself will be made to submit to some unbiblical principle of interpretation. The way the tide runs at present within the movement is not encouraging. To avoid a head-on collision between two really incompatible axioms—that some biblical facts must be given up on critical grounds, but that the biblical outlook must be retained on grounds of faith—its adherents have devised ways whereby the meaning of factual statements in Scripture may be preserved without any factual reference being ascribed to them. One way is by using the concept of 'myth', which has become very significant in modern theology. By 'myth' is meant a quasi-factual narrative which, despite its form, is intended only to tell us some truth about our own lives in the present without giving us any information about external events, past or future. 'Myths' tell us nothing of happenings in the physical world, but leave us free to speculate about them as we will. This concept is commonly applied to the stories of the creation and the fall, which, it is said, are meant to teach us, not that there was a first man who was made good and sinned, but simply that we ourselves are God's creatures and are sinners—'Adam is Everyman'.[1] Bultmann, a radical if ever there was one, treats the whole New Testament witness to the Person and work of Christ—His pre-existence, virgin birth, deity, sinlessness, atoning death, resurrection, ascension, and future return to judgment—as just a complex myth. It means, he tells us, not that these things happened, but that there is now open to man a new 'possibility of existence'—that of letting go the past (= dying with Christ) and opening oneself to the future (= rising with Christ); and to embrace it brings inner release (=salvation).[2] Few go as far as Bultmann, but most theologians today use the category of 'myth' to erode the factual reference of biblical statements at some point or other.

Then, too, neo-orthodoxy has developed in various forms the distinction between the Bible as the fallible word of man and the infallible word which God speaks through it, but which is at no point identical with it—a distinction which, at least if it is developed logically, seems to turn Christianity into mysticism. Biblical sanction for either of these devices seems to be wholly lacking. The introduction of them has encouraged theologians to make great play with biblical categories without committing themselves to any genuine acceptance of the biblical world-view; in

[1] A. Richardson in *A Theological Word-book of the Bible* (S.C.M., 1950), s.v. 'Adam'; quoted by Hebert, *op. cit.*, p. 39. (Hebert himself does not agree with this.)

[2] See P. E. Hughes, *Scripture and Myth* (Tyndale Press, 1956), pp. 7, 11, etc. Bultmann goes on to advocate dropping the mythological mode of stating this 'meaning'.

that way, these concepts have opened a new road back into the subjectivist morass out of which 'Biblical Theology' hoped to escape. They must be adjudged sterile sophistications; and it is a matter for regret that 'Biblical Theology' today should be found invoking their aid to prop itself up on shifting sand, rather than labouring to clear away all remnants of subjectivism and so reach a rock foundation at last.

The 'Biblical Theologian' is thus a modern Mr. Facing-both-ways; and Evangelicals cannot be expected to commit themselves to him till the inner ambiguity of his position is resolved. Spokesmen of this movement often seem surprised and pained that Evangelicals should treat their overtures so coolly, when (they protest) the two groups hold so many truths in common. But until 'Biblical Theology' has accepted the principle of biblical authority without reserve or equivocation, Evangelicals cannot tell whether the two groups mean the same thing by their common confession or not. Until 'Biblical Theologians' cease to hunt for question-begging formulæ on the authority issue (such as 'the authority of the gospel', which Hebert and others favour), and acknowledge the method of exposition and reformation to be the only permissible procedure in Christian theology, no common ground can be known to exist. It is scarcely unreasonable, in the circumstances, for Evangelicals to require some guarantee that this ambiguous theology is not a form of subjectivism in disguise; nor to hold aloof when it turns out that no such guarantee is forthcoming.

BAD CHRISTIANITY

We do not question the sincerity of any Liberal; but if we were developing a critique of liberal theology, we should argue, on the basis of our reasoning thus far, that Liberalism is faulty in the following fundamental ways:

1. *It discounts the authority of Christ.* As we saw, Christ taught the principle of biblical authority quite unambiguously. Any sort of subjectivism, therefore, involves rejecting His authority as a teacher at this point. We showed that it is impossible to argue that Christ did

not intend to endorse the authority of Scripture, and unwarrantable to suppose that He did not mean this part of His teaching to bind His disciples, or that He was the victim of false notions here. Liberalism declares in effect that Christ was wrong, and labours to correct Him. But by what right may a disciple thus patronize his Master? 'Why call ye me, Lord, Lord, and do not the things which I say?'[1]

2. *Liberalism expresses an attitude of intellectual impenitence.* Repentance means a change of mind; part of which, as we saw, is the abandoning of the sinful quest for intellectual autonomy and the recognition that true wisdom begins with a willingness to treat God's Word as possessing final authority. Repentance means renouncing the pride which would hail man as the measure of all things, and embracing the humility of the little child who knows his ignorance, wants to learn and is ready to be taught. But subjectivism, which makes human judgment the arbiter of divine truth, is just an expression of this pride. Its persistence in Christians is as much a besetting sin as is any weakness of conduct. Pride, unrecognized, unforsaken and unmortified, lies at the root of it. This sometimes becomes very plain when we hear anti-fundamentalists rebuking Evangelicals for their obscurantism and congratulating themselves on their own fancied enlightenment. We do not and dare not claim that Evangelicals are in fact free from the canker of intellectual pride. 'Who can discern his errors? . . . Keep back thy servant also from presumptuous sins; let them not have dominion over me.'[2] But we would insist that intellectual penitence and humility are at least possible on evangelical principles, whereas on liberal principles they are not even that.

3. *Liberalism denies the rule of the Creator over His world.* Its various revisions of biblical history, little as they agree in other respects, are at one in this: that they always whittle down the supernatural element. The liberal doctrine of 'progressive revelation' and of the inspiration of Scripture reduces the divine control over man at every

[1] Lk. vi. 46. [2] Ps. xix. 12, 13, RV.

point; God, it is said, *could not help* misunderstandings and untruths creeping into the minds of His prophets and the records of His revelation, because He had to take human material as He found it! But is this the Scripture doctrine of Scripture? And by what right may we speak in this blithe way of 'him who worketh all things after the counsel of his own will'?[1] Liberalism pictures a world in which God's influence is always remote and never decisive; which is not the biblical view. By trying to combine the Christian message with the idea of a material world in which God, so far from being sovereign, is a stranger, liberal theology reveals itself to be the heir of Gnosticism rather than of Christianity.

4. *Liberalism presupposes an apologetic strategy which is radically wrong.* This point requires development.

When the nineteenth century began, educated Europe was drifting from Christianity; for rationalistic Deism had made men sceptical of the supernaturalism of Scripture. From Schleiermacher, its founder, down to the present, therefore, liberal theology has had an apologetic motive. But its apologetic strategy has been based on two errors.

In the first place, Liberalism always imagined that the less there was to defend, the easier it would be to defend it. Non-essentials, it was said, may be jettisoned without loss; we need not maintain the accuracy of all Bible history, or the reality of all Bible miracles, or the truth of all Bible teaching; we need only fight for 'the essential Christian message'. This, of course, brought in subjectivism straight away; for who was to say what this 'essential Christian message' was? And in any case the supposition is false. The Christian revelation is a complete world-view, supernatural from first to last. It makes a connected and intelligible whole; but, being supernatural, it does not at any point admit of demonstrative proof. As we showed, it is not unreasonable—indeed, it is wisdom—to believe the whole on God's authority; and if we do, our faith in each part will be strengthened as we reflect on its congruity with the rest. Thus, it is not hard to believe in the virgin birth when one believes that Jesus

[1] Eph. i. 11.

was God incarnate, nor hard to believe that Jesus was God incarnate when one believes in God as Creator, nor hard to believe in the inspiration of an infallible Scripture, or in any other miraculous happening, when one believes in a Creator who is sovereign and does whatever He pleases in heaven and in earth. But it would be wholly unreasonable to accept part of this supernatural faith on God's authority and reject the rest on one's own authority, merely because one lacked demonstrative proof of it. To accept all is consistent; to reject all is consistent; but no third course is consistent. To profess to retain the 'essential Christian message' while rejecting the lesser miracles is utterly inconsistent. And to make a convincing defence of an expurgated Christianity, so far from being comparatively easy, is absolutely impossible; for the position to be defended is intrinsically unreasonable. If man's judgment is to be the measure of some things in Scripture, why not of all things? If we are entitled to desupernaturalize the faith in part, why not altogether? It is hard to respect the liberal half-way houses, however much acuteness and learning goes into their erection; for they are arbitrary through and through. These compromise Christianities have been preached for a century now, and we can judge of their effects : their apologetic value had been negligible, and their effect in the churches has been so to weaken men's faith in the sovereign majesty of God that it is now necessary for Canon J. B. Phillips to write a book for churchpeople entitled *Your God is Too Small.* It is Liberalism within the churches, as much as any influence outside them, that has so reduced our ideas of Him. It is ironical that a movement which was expected to increase the Church's impact on the world outside should have had the effect of a Fifth Column, undermining its faith from within; but so it has been. Shrunken Christianities always have this effect. History shows that Christian witness is strong and effective only when believers are humble enough to believe nothing less about God than His own Word tells us.

In the second place, Liberalism misconceived the bearing of historical enquiry on faith. 'History', of course, is a word with two meanings: it refers both to past events themselves and to the historian's investigation of them and verdicts about them. Now, we do not dispute that Christian faith rests on history in the first sense. The Christian message is essentially a declaration of God's saving deeds in history. Acts of God are the facts of faith; and if the facts fall, faith falls with them. Thus, 'if Christ be not raised, your faith is vain; ye are yet in your sins'.[1] The ground of faith in these facts, however, is sure; it is that God has vouched for them in His Word. The fact that Scripture records events is sufficient proof that they happened; the veracity of God is our guarantee. And our historical investigation of Scripture should be such as expresses faith in God's veracity: we should assume the truth of the record as the basis for enquiry into its meaning. This, as we have seen, is the authentic Christian approach.

Liberalism, however, deviated from this by maintaining that faith must rest on history in a different sense: namely, that our beliefs should be circumscribed by the conclusions of historical enquiry into the truth of Scripture, proceeding on the assumption that God has not, after all, guaranteed its accuracy. The nineteenth century prided itself on having perfected the technique of 'scientific' history—a rigorous discipline for evaluating documentary sources. Liberalism, a child of the 'scientific' age, thought itself bound, as a matter of intellectual honesty, to capitulate to the claim that 'scientific' history alone gives sure knowledge of past events. The Liberals concluded that they must therefore submit the biblical documents to the scrutiny of the new method, and treat them henceforth exactly like non-biblical documents of similar sorts—setting up none as infallible, but giving more weight to first-hand contemporary material than to what seems second-hand and remote in time, less to accounts that appear to be written 'with a moral' than to those that do not, and so on. And faith, they held, must abide by the results of this scrutiny, whatever these may be. What this meant was that the 'scientific' historian must

[1] 1 Cor. xv. 17.

have passed the historical narratives of Scripture as providing (by his standards) 'good' evidence for thinking that the events recorded really happened, before we may even raise the question, whether we should regard them in the way that Scripture does—as acts of God, and therefore as objects of faith. The 'Biblical Theologians' see, more clearly than earlier Liberals did, that faith is something quite distinct from a mere historical judgment as to the possibility of certain stories' being true; but this only makes them more insistent that, until such an historical judgment is forthcoming, the question of faith cannot legitimately come up. Thus, Hebert draws the following conclusion from his review of the resurrection narratives: 'That if the Resurrection is true, it is just such narratives as these that would bear fitting testimony to it.' ('Fitting' is as far as the judgment of the critical historian can take us.) 'And *if* the narratives do in fact stand up to such an interrogation of them,' Hebert continues, '*then* it remains for each individual to make his response of faith.'[1] But if not—then, presumably, the question would never arise. The possibility of faith thus rests entirely on the historian's verdict.[2]

If this approach is right, it leads us to the odd conclusion that the Church's faith rested on a wrong foundation for the first eighteen hundred years of its life, but that this could not be corrected till the technique of 'scientific

[1] *Op. cit.*, p. 83, our italics.

[2] Kidner (*loc. cit.*) calls attention to this implication of the sentence from Hebert last quoted in the text. 'It is instructive to observe where the conditional clause comes. . . . This is no accident of phraseology, for he has already owned that if the resurrection story had been given only in a single, well-turned narrative, or had attempted descriptions of our Lord's appearance, etc., we might well have had to judge it an artificial construction. Yet it *could* have been reported in such terms, with perfect veracity. The true story would not have *rung* true, and the historian would have withheld belief as conscientiously as Doubting Thomas.' And what should the Church do when (as happens) some reputable historians deny that the resurrection stories as they stand ring true? Why should we be guided by the verdict that Hebert would doubtless pass on them, rather than by that which they would doubtless pass on Hebert? Such considerations make plain the bottomless subjectivism of this method.

history' was worked out a century ago. Moreover, it prompts the question : on what grounds are we being exhorted to make our 'response of faith' to the biblical claim that Christ rose from the dead? The ground is evidently not the historian's verdict, for that is merely a pronouncement that for all he knows, it may have been so. Nor can it be the fact that Scripture affirms it, for that by itself is not sufficient ground for believing anything; if we need the historian to tell us whether the Scripture story could possibly be true it would clearly be unreasonable to ask us to believe that it actually is true, just because Scripture relates it. Nor can the ground for faith be the fact that the Church has always believed in the resurrection; the fact that we have to appeal to the historian to say if such belief is permissible shows that the Church's historic testimony is in no way decisive. What, then, is the ground of faith? 'Biblical Theologians' seem unable, or unwilling, to tell us; but it seems that, on their own principles, they must think of it as some inner impulse that does not correspond to any objective basis for certainty. In that case, however, it is clear that Dr. Ramsey's phrases about 'abdicating the use of your mind' and 'a will to leap in the dark' perfectly sum up the evangelistic message of 'Biblical Theology'.

But in fact this approach is not right. Faith does not wait on historical criticism. Certainly, there is value in reviewing the quantity and strength of the evidence that there is (regarded simply as human testimony) for the great Christian facts. It is good to test the credentials of Christianity by the most searching scholarship, and to make faith give account of itself at the bar of history; for thereby its intellectual adequacy is made to appear. To show in this way that faith is not unreasonable helps to confirm believers and to remove stumbling-blocks from before others. In 1 Cor. xv. 5 ff., Paul reviews the human testimony to the resurrection in order to strengthen his readers' faith. But, as he pointed out earlier in that letter (and as we showed in Chapter V of this book), faith is not founded on human testimony, or on any merely human judgment at all. 'When first I came to Corinth,'

Paul wrote, 'my speech and my preaching were not in persuasive words of wisdom'—not the wisdom of the philosopher, nor yet of the historian—'but in demonstration of the Spirit and of power: that your faith should not stand in the wisdom of men, but in the power of God.'[1] Paul preached his gospel as a message from God—truth which God had revealed to him, and which he now proclaimed 'in words which the Holy Ghost teacheth'—and faith meant, as it still means, receiving that message, 'not as the word of men, but as it is in truth, the word of God, which effectually worketh also in you that believe.'[2] Faith is rooted in the realization that the gospel is God's word; and faith recognizes in its divine origin a full and sufficient guarantee of its veracity. So with Scripture, 'God's Word written': faith rests its confidence in the truth of biblical narratives, not on the critical acumen of the historian, but on the unfailing trustworthiness of God.[3]

And the honest way to commend God's revealed truth to an unbelieving generation is not to disguise it as a word of man, and to act as if we could never be sure of it, but had to keep censoring and amending it at the behest of the latest scholarship, and dared not believe it further than historical agnosticism gives us leave; but to preach it in a way which shows the world that we believe it wholeheartedly, and to cry to God to accompany our witness

[1] See 1 Cor. ii. 4, 5, RV.

[2] 1 Thes. ii. 13.

[3] It should perhaps be emphasized that we do not mean by this that Scripture history is written according to the canons of modern scientific history. Biblical historians are not concerned to answer all the questions which modern historians ask, nor to tell their story with the detailed completeness to which the modern researcher aspires. It is no more possible to write a full history of Israel from the Old Testament documents than to write a complete biography of Christ from the four Gospels, or a full record of the expansion of Christianity during its first thirty years from Acts. The biblical writers had their own aims and interests guiding their selection of the evidence, and their own conventions for using it; and if we fail to take account of these things in interpreting what they wrote, we violate the canon of literal interpretation: cf. pp. 102 ff. above. Our point in the text is simply that, when Scripture professes to narrate fact, faith receives the narrative as factual on God's authority, and does not conclude it to be legendary, or mythical, or mistaken, or mere human authority.

with His Spirit, so that we too may preach 'in demonstration of the Spirit and of power'. The apologetic strategy that would attract converts by the flattery of accommodating the gospel to the 'wisdom' of sinful man was condemned by Paul nineteen centuries ago, and the past hundred years have provided a fresh demonstration of its bankruptcy. The world may call its compromises 'progressive' and 'enlightened' (those are its names for all forms of thought that pander to its conceit); those who produce them will doubtless, by a natural piece of wishful thinking, call them 'bold' and 'courageous', and perhaps 'realistic' and 'wholesome'; but the Bible condemns them as sterile aberrations. And the Church cannot hope to recover its power till it resolves to turn its back on them.

CHAPTER VIII

CONCLUSION

And Elijah came unto all the people, and said, How long halt ye between two opinions? if the Lord be God, follow him.

1 KINGS xviii. 21

But this I admit to you, that according to the Way, which they call a sect, I worship the God of our fathers, believing everything laid down by the law or written in the prophets.

ACTS xxiv. 14, RSV

OUR argument is done, and it only remains to draw the threads together. Let us sum up what we have tried to say.

We have traced the history and meaning of the word 'Fundamentalism', and concluded that, because of its prejudicial character, and associations, it is not a useful title for Evangelicals today.

We have expounded the biblical doctrine of biblical authority, and shown that the belief and behaviour of Christian men must be controlled and directed throughout by the teaching of Scripture. To rest content with the guidance of unreformed Church tradition, or uncriticized private opinion, not tested by the written Word, is theologically illegitimate, and Scripture warns us against lapses of this sort.

We have examined the Biblical concept of Scripture, and found that the Bible asks to be regarded as a God-given, error-free, self-interpreting unity, true and trustworthy in all that it teaches. We have seen, too, that the factor which is decisive in the creating of faith in Scripture is not the witness of any one theologian or group of theologians, nor even of the whole historic Church, but the witness of the Holy Spirit, its divine Author, who teaches Christians both to trust it as the Word of God and to understand its meaning.

We have studied the relation of reason to faith, and

shown that the proper role of reason is to express faith by receiving, applying and transmitting revealed truth. We have seen that faith and reason only come into conflict when reason defies God's authority, refuses to be a servant of faith, and reverts to some sort of unbelief; and we have observed that the much-vaunted 'freedom' which reason thus gains is actually perfect slavery.

We have applied all this to Liberalism, both in its older form and in its modern dress ('Biblical Theology'), and shown that this approach to the Scriptures is not merely unscientific and uncritical, but sinful and self-contradictory too.

THE SIGNIFICANCE OF THIS CONTROVERSY

Our argument has shown the real nature of the choice with which this debate confronts us. It is not a choice between obscurantism and scholarship, nor between crudeness and sensitivity in biblical exposition. It concerns quite a different issue, and a far deeper one, although critics of Evangelicalism rarely seem to see it, or if they do, are shy of discussing it. The fact is that here we are faced in principle with a choice between two versions of Christianity. It is a choice between historic Evangelicalism and modern Subjectivism; between a Christianity that is consistent with itself and one that is not; in effect, between one that is wholly God-given and one that is partly man-made. We have to choose whether to bow to the authority claimed by the Son of God, or whether on our own authority to discount and contravene a part of His teaching; whether to rest content with Christianity according to Christ, or whether to go hankering after a Christianity according to the spirit of our age; whether to behave as Christ's disciples, or as His tutors. We have to choose whether we will accept the biblical doctrine of Scripture as it stands, or permit ourselves to re-fashion it according to our fancy. We have to choose whether to embrace the delusion that human creatures are competent to judge and find fault with the words of their Creator, or whether to recognize this idea for the blasphemy that it is and drop it. We have to decide whether we are going to carry through our repentance on the intellectual level, or whether we shall still cherish our sinful craving for a thought-life free from the rule of God. We have to decide whether it is right to make such an idol of nineteenth-century biblical criticism that not even God is allowed to touch it. We have to decide whether to say that we believe the Bible and mean it, or to look for ways whereby we can say it without having to accept all the consequences. We have to choose whether to allow the sovereign Spirit to teach us faith in Scripture as such, or whether to appeal to historians to delimit the area of scriptural assertion within which faith is permissible. We have to choose whether, in presenting Christianity to others, we are going to rely on the demonstration of the Spirit to commend it, or on our own ability to make it masquerade as the fulfilment of secular thought. Evangelicals have made their choice on all these issues. What their critics are really asking them to do is to reverse it: to enter into a marriage of convenience with Subjectivism. But Evangelicals cannot in conscience consent to being thus mis-mated.

Evangelicals, indeed, are bound to oppose Subjectivism as vigorously as they can. They must do so, in the first place, because subjectivist principles, if consistently worked out, would totally destroy supernatural Christianity. If the human mind is set up as the measure and test of truth, it will quickly substitute for man's incomprehensible Creator a comprehensible idol fashioned in man's own image; man wants a god he can manage and feel comfortable with, and will inevitably invent one if allowed.[1] He will forget (because he cannot understand) the infinite gulf that separates the Creator from His creatures, and will picture to himself a god wholly involved in this world and wholly comprehensible (in principle, at any rate) by the speculative intellect. It was no accident, but a natural development, that made the liberal theology of the last century so strongly pantheistic. Once men reverse the proper relation between Scripture and their own thinking and start judging biblical statements about God by their

[1] Cf. Rom. i. 20–25.

private ideas of God, instead of *vice versa*, their knowledge of the Creator is in imminent danger of perishing, and with it the whole idea of supernatural redemption. If they were consistent, it would perish; if in fact they remain Christians, this is despite their principles, not because of them. The preservation of the Christian knowledge of God therefore requires that all forms of Subjectivism be relentlessly opposed—including Liberalism, both ancient and modern. It is true that 'Biblical Theology' speaks as if it hopes to climb out of the subjectivist sea, but the 'critical' approach to the Bible is like a millstone round its neck, and seems likely to pull it back in. Until 'Biblical Theology' convincingly disavows Subjectivism, Evangelicals cannot regard it as a friend; and Subjectivism itself must be regarded as an enemy, wherever and in whatever guise it is found.

Then, in the second place, even when it stops short of destroying Christianity altogether, Subjectivism perverts the nature of it as a religion of grace. It is one aspect of a twofold movement which has created conflict in the Church since its beginning. The basic cause of this conflict is that sinful man would like to change the character of Christianity. Christianity is a religion of divine grace—one, that is, which declares that it is God's sovereign prerogative to give, and that man's part is only to receive. Salvation, with all that it involves, comes to man by faith; and faith is no more than an activity of reception, contributing nothing to that which it receives. Nor is there need for man to contribute to the saving gifts of God; for they are perfect in themselves, and are all that man requires. But to admit the truth of this is humbling, for it leaves man nothing to do for which he can claim credit; and sinners are proud. Hence professed Christians are tempted to pander to their pride by trying to find a way in which, after all, they can contribute something to their own salvation. These attempts are made along two main avenues; that of works, for securing acceptance with God, and that of ideas, for explicating and qualifying God's revealed truth. Both tendencies were manifested in New Testament times; Paul wrote his Epistle to the Galatians against a Judaizing Christianity which was a form of the first, and that to the

Colossians against a Gnostic Christianity which was a form of the second.

The Reformers, confronted by the first tendency as it appeared in the mediæval system of meritorious works and priestly sacrifices, saw how to combat it: they condemned the system because it obscured the unique glory of Christ's perfect priesthood and sacrifice, and set men to do for themselves what Christ had done for them already. Today, the heirs of the Reformers must oppose the second tendency, as it appears in the liberal approach to revelation, on precisely similar grounds. Liberalism, as we saw, sets us the task of sorting out the divine utterances from the total mass of Scripture by the exercise of our own wits, guided in part by extra-biblical principles of judgment. But in this, again, we are being told to do for ourselves what Christ has done for us already. Christ located the utterance of God for us once and for all; it is Scripture, as such. That being so, it is not for us to pick and choose within Scripture, or to bring speculative principles to bear on Scripture, any more than we should go about to establish our own righteousness; instead, we should bow before God's written revelation without more ado, just as we should submit forthwith to the righteousness of God in the gospel. Our part is simply to receive what God graciously gives—a perfect righteousness in the one case, a perfect revelation in the other. Liberalism, like all Subjectivism, discounts the perfection and truth of Scripture in order to make room for man to contribute his own ideas to his knowledge of God, just as Mediævalism discounted the perfection of Christ's merits in order to make room for man to contribute his own merits to his acceptance with God. But Christ's merits do not need to be augmented by human works; and God's revealed truth does not need to be edited, cut, corrected and improved by the cleverness of man. To attempt either task is to insult God (by denying the perfection of His gifts) and to flatter ourselves (by supposing that we can improve on them). The only right attitude for us is to confess that our works are vile and our wisdom foolishness, and to receive with thankfulness the flawless righteousness and the perfect Scriptures which

God in mercy gives us. Anything else is a conceited affront to divine grace. And evangelical theology is bound to oppose the attitude which under-values the gift of Scripture and presumes to correct the inerrant Word of God, just as it will oppose all misguided endeavours to supplement by human merit the perfect righteousness of Christ.

It is evident, in the light of all this, that the allegation that Evangelicalism is sectarian, schismatic and un-catholic in its outlook is wide of the mark. Hebert, not seeing the doctrinal issues underlying its controversy with the rest of Christendom, equates the evangelical attitude (by innuendo, at any rate) with the party-spirit fomented by the personality-cult at Corinth.[1] But in fact Evangelicalism is the truest Catholicism; and the controversy which it maintains against Subjectivism (and Traditionalism too) is the clearest proof of this. After all, there is no other standard of catholicity save Christ Himself; and the dimensions of catholicity are first theological and then historical, and not numerical at all. The catholicity of Evangelicalism appears, first, in its uncompromising submission to the teaching of Christ and of Scripture on authority, as on all other matters, and, second, in its oneness with all those who down the ages have taken this same position, bowing to the authority of Scripture, glorying in the biblical gospel of free grace, and contending earnestly for the apostolic faith. Those who are conscious of standing with Augustine, Luther, Calvin, Baxter, Owen, Wesley, Whitefield, Edwards; with the Reformers, Huguenots, Puritans, Covenanters; with the Evangelicals of the eighteenth century and the architects of the world missionary movement in the nineteenth—to mention no more—such need not fear for their catholicity. Evangelicals may seem no more than a dissentient minority in the present-day Church, but this is no new state of affairs; Luther once seemed to be in a minority of one; so did Elijah, and Jeremiah, and Paul. Indeed, there are comparatively few periods in history when Evangelicals have been more than a dissentient minority within a larger group, meeting indifference, if not unfriendliness, from

[1] *Op. cit.*, pp. 117 ff.

fellow-members of their churches. But true catholicism is not a matter of being in the biggest party. Numerically, the unreformed Church of Rome is the biggest party; but many anti-fundamentalists would no doubt agree with four centuries of Protestant theology that the self-styled 'Catholic Church' is in fact the biggest schismatic group in Christendom. It is often said that one with God is a majority, however many stand against him; and it is no less true that one with Christ is a catholic Christian, however many deny his right to the title.

THE LESSONS OF THIS CONTROVERSY

What should Evangelicals do in face of the current criticisms? We would mention three things.

First, we must humbly and honestly examine ourselves in the light of the strictures that have been passed on our practice. What they suggest is that we have not in fact lived under the authority of Scripture as conscientiously as we should have done. We may quote here from a review of Hebert's book by an evangelical writer:

'As a display of certain evangelical prejudices and idiosyncrasies, the book might well make many loyal Evangelicals sit up and do some salutary thinking. There *is* a place for repentance in the Christian life, both for moral waywardness and intellectual stubbornness . . .

'. . . There is more than one shrewd blow against the ultra-subjective nature of much evangelical preaching, devotion and living. In places, evangelical life *is* superficial and rootless, lacking the stability which a historical tradition can give'—although, he adds, 'if Evangelicals lack a sense of their glorious heritage, that is not because the heritage does not exist . . .

'Then we readily admit that much evangelical worship is slipshod, and sometimes even downright irreverent. This may be partly due to our excessive preoccupation with children's work. Many never move on to the richness and depth of adult Christianity . . . The majesty and glory of "gospel worship" (as our forefathers termed it) is often missing . . . The answer is . . . the recovery of the dignity of the evangelical message itself—the greatness of the gospel which the minister preaches, the hymns enshrine, and the prayers dwell upon in adoration, thanksgiving and petition . . .'[1]

There is no doubt that we need to put our house in order. And if the current spate of criticism moves us to do so, then the 'Fundamentalism controversy' will have done immense good in invigorating the evangelical cause.

Second, we must keep before us the real issues in this debate, and try to keep discussion centred upon them. As we saw, the critics of Evangelicalism are anxious to give the impression that serious doctrinal issues are not involved at all; but we have shown that this is the very reverse of the truth. We have seen what the real issues are: the authority of Christ and of Scripture; the relation between the Bible and reason; the method of theology, and the meaning of repentance; the choice between Evangelicalism and Subjectivism. Until agreement is reached on these matters, it is profitless to start discussing the other subjects—the doctrine of the Church, for instance, or the nature of the atonement—which have come up in the course of the controversy. First principles must be first dealt with. Evangelicals should not let themselves be intimidated by the shower of explosive words—'Fundamentalist', 'obscurantist', 'literalist' and the rest—that is regularly poured out upon them. They should request a reasoned statement of the accusations preferred against them, and offer a reasoned defence of their position in terms of their own first principles. That defence, no doubt, will involve some kind of criticism of the position of their accusers—as it has done in this book. But this is as it should be. For Evangelicals are bound, as servants of God and disciples of Christ, to oppose Subjectivism wherever they find it. Defending truth, and exposing error, are two aspects of the same task.

Third, we ought to take courage. When Evangelicalism can be ignored, it is weak; when it is no longer possible to ignore it, it is certainly growing stronger. The fact that the present controversy is in progress at all is a testimony

[1] O. R. Johnston, in *The Theological Students' Fellowship Terminal Letter*, Autumn 1957, pp. 12 f.

to renewed vitality in evangelical circles. For it is the nature of the gospel to create controversy; and the vigour with which the gospel is spoken against is an index of the faithfulness and power with which it is being preached. And so we would end this book by quoting and applying to the present situation some words written by Machen a generation ago, at an earlier stage in this conflict :

'Let us not fear the opposition of men : every great movement in the Church from Paul down to modern times has been criticized on the ground that it promoted censoriousness and intolerance and disputing. Of course the gospel of Christ, in a world of sin and doubt, will cause disputing; and if it does not cause disputing and arouse bitter opposition, that is a fairly sure sign that it is not being faithfully proclaimed. As for me, I believe that a great opportunity has been opened to Christian people by the "controversy" that is so much decried. Conventions have been broken down; men are trying to penetrate beneath pious words to the thing that these words designate; it is becoming increasingly necessary for a man to choose whether he will stand with Christ or against Him. Such a condition, I for my part believe, has been brought about by the Spirit of God; already there has been genuine spiritual advance . . . And God grant that His fire be not quenched ! God save us from any smoothing over of these questions in the interests of a hollow pleasantness; God grant that great questions of principle may never rest until they are settled right ! It is out of such times of questioning that great revivals come. God grant that it may be so today ! Controversy of the right sort is good; for out of such controversy, as Church history and Scripture alike teach, there comes the salvation of souls.'[1]

[1] *What is Faith?*, pp. 41 ff.

APPENDIX I

PROFESSOR ALAN RICHARDSON ON 'FUNDAMENTALISM'

THE short article on 'Fundamentalism' in the 1950 edition of *Chambers' Encyclopædia* is extraordinarily misleading. Dr. D. Johnson remarked on its inaccuracy in his article, 'The Word "Fundamentalist"', in the *Christian Graduate* for March 1955 (p. 22), but it still stands unchanged in the 1957 edition. It is worth examining in some detail, partly because it is typical of much present-day misconception, and partly because, appearing where it does, it is likely to be used as an authority for more.

Dr. Richardson, as we saw,[1] defines 'Fundamentalism' as a theory of the mode of biblical inspiration 'which regards the written words of the Bible as divinely dictated'. As Dr. Johnson pointed out, a definition that refers only to the 'fundamentalist' view of Scripture is too narrow to fit the historical facts; in any case, the view stated by Dr. Richardson was never the 'fundamentalist' view of Scripture at all, as we shall now see.

This theory, we are told, 'was developed by way of reaction' to nineteenth-century biblical criticism; it 'represents a hardening of the traditional pre-critical view . . . that the Spirit of God had miraculously communicated the truths of revelation to the biblical writers, though the manner of this communication had never been precisely defined by the Church'. What evidence is there for this 'hardening'? None at all. The fact is that Protestant defenders of the divine origin of the Bible during the past century have uniformly been at pains to disclaim any mechanical doctrine of the mode of inspiration, to stress that the biblical authors wrote spontaneously and freely, and to insist that the product of their writing is as truly

[1] P. 10 above.

and fully human as it is divine. See, for example, W. Lee, *The Inspiration of the Holy Scriptures* (2nd ed., 1857), pp. 21 ff.; C. Wordsworth, *The Inspiration of the Bible* (1861), p. 5; L. Gaussen, *Theopneustia,* Eng. tr. by David Scott (1863), III. i. 3, 23–26, pp. 107, 125 f.; C. Hodge, *Systematic Theology* (1873), I, 156 f.; W. Cunningham. *Theological Lectures* (1878), pp. 349 ff.; W. B. Pope, *Compendium of Christian Theology* (2nd ed., 1879), I. 171, 183; A. A. Hodge, *Outlines of Theology* (2nd ed., 1883), Chapter IV; C. H. Waller, *Authoritative Inspiration* (1887), pp. 200 f.; J. C. Ryle, *Old Paths* (4th ed., 1895), pp. 17 f.; H. C. G. Moule, *Veni Creator* (1890), pp. 53 f.; A. H. Strong, *Systematic Theology* (12th ed., 1949), pp. 208 ff.; J. Orr, *Revelation and Inspiration* (1909), p. 210; B. B. Warfield, *The Inspiration and Authority of the Bible* (re-issued 1951), pp. 153 ff. Of these, only Cunningham and Gaussen use the metaphor of 'dictation' at all, and they qualify it with great care. Lee and Orr prefer to speak of 'plenary', and Strong of 'dynamical', inspiration rather than use the term 'verbal', which they fear is too closely linked with mechanical ideas. The mechanical view of inspiration is explicitly disclaimed in *The Fundamentals*[1]; Hebert notes that T. C. Hammond disowns it,[2] and rightly affirms that the theory is 'repudiated by all the conservative evangelical leaders'.[3] So it always has been. The 'dictation-theory' is a theological mare's-nest; it never existed at any time during the past century save in certain people's imagination. In 1893 B. B. Warfield wrote : 'It ought to be unnecessary to protest again against the habit of representing the advocates of "verbal inspiration" as teaching that the mode of inspiration was by dictation.'[4] Still less ought it to be necessary in 1958—but hoary error dies hard.

Dr. Richardson goes on to quote, as a 'classical statement' of 'Fundamentalism', part of the peroration of a sermon preached by J. W. Burgon at Oxford in 1860 (not 1861, as Richardson says)—some sixty years, we observe,

[1] 1917 ed., II. 16 (J. M. Gray).

[2] *Op. cit.*, p. 60, quoting T. C. Hammond, *Inspiration and Authority*, p. 23.

[3] P. 56.

[4] *The Inspiration and Authority of the Bible*, p. 173 n.

before the term 'Fundamentalism' was coined. We subjoin the complete passage.[1] 'The Bible is none other than *the voice of Him that sitteth upon the Throne*! Every book of it, every chapter of it, every verse of it, every word of it, every syllable of it (where are we to stop?), every letter of it, is the direct utterance of the Most High! *Pasa graphē theopneustos.*[2] "Well spake the Holy Ghost, by the mouth of" the many blessed men who wrote it. The Bible is none other than *the Word of God;* not some part of it, more, some part of it, less; but all alike, the utterance of Him that sitteth upon the Throne; absolute, faultless, unerring, supreme.' This is nothing more than a rhetorical affirmation of the divine origin of all Scripture. Burgon is affirming the fact of inspiration; he is not discussing the mode of it, and the passage contains not a word to suggest that dictation was the method whereby Scripture was given. Indeed, a few pages further on Burgon explicitly repudiates the construction which Dr. Richardson puts on his words. ('Let me not be told . . . that this is to advocate a mechanical theory . . . I should as soon think of holding a theory of Providence and Free-will, as of holding a theory of Inspiration . . . Inspiration,—the analysis of which is so favourite a problem with this inquisitive age,—is far, far, above us. . . . The method of Inspiration is . . . one of the many things I cannot fully understand, much less pretend to explain.'[3]) So much for the 'classical statement' of 'Fundamentalism'!

Dr. Richardson continues: 'Such views are now abandoned in the theological faculties of British Universities.' If this means the views attributed to Burgon, we must insist that they were never held, in British Universities or any other. If, however, the statement had been intended to imply that no theological teachers in British Universities today maintain the historic Christian view of inspiration which Burgon in fact held, it would be simply false.

Dr. Richardson concludes by saying that 'Fundamentalism' flourished chiefly in America. This in the context

[1] J. W. Burgon, *Inspiration and Interpretation*, 1905 reprint, p. 86.
[2] 2 Tim. iii. 16, the text of Burgon's sermon.
[3] *Op. cit.*, pp. 112–114.

of the article suggests that American Fundamentalists contended for the 'dictation-theory'. But this was not so; what they stood for was the fact of inspiration, not any theory as to the method of it; and, as we have shown, they stood for much more besides, which Dr. Richardson nowhere mentions.

It seems a pity that such a misleading account of this matter should find a place in a standard work of reference.

APPENDIX II

DR. HEBERT ON PSEUDONYMITY IN SCRIPTURE

THE aim of this note is not to discuss any specific cases of alleged pseudonymous authorship of biblical books, but to clarify the general evangelical view on this subject in the light of Hebert's confusing discussion of the position taken by the *New Bible Commentary*.

Hebert thinks that the Commentary is both unreasonable, in ruling out *a priori* the possibility that some biblical books are not by the authors whose names they bear, and also inconsistent in applying its own principles; for, he says, 'the principle of pseudonymity is admitted . . . in the case of Ecclesiastes.'[1] This is not so. The principle of pseudonymity, in the sense in which the Commentary rejects it, is involved only when a book seeks to impose itself upon its readers as being by someone other than its real author. The view of Ecclesiastes taken by the Commentary is explicitly stated in the note on Ec. i. 1 : 'The author does not really claim to be Solomon but places his words in Solomon's mouth'; this device 'was not intended to deceive anyone, and none of its original readers would in fact have been deceived'.[2] The literary character of the book is unambiguous; the Preacher is transparently not Solomon, just as parables are transparently not history, and the form of his sermon (a meditation put into Solomon's mouth) no more involves an assertion of Solomonic authorship than the narrative form of Christ's story of the Good Samaritan involves an assertion that the events recounted actually happened. The principle of pseudonymity does not arise here, any more than it does when an article in a religious weekly begins : 'I am a collection-bag.'[3]

[1] *Op. cit.*, p. 91. [2] *New Bible Commentary*, p. 539.

[3] For a fuller defence of this view of Ecclesiastes by an evangelical scholar, see E. J. Young, *Introduction to the Old Testament*, pp. 339 f.

Hebert goes on to affirm it 'strange' for A. M. Stibbs to write that, since 'documents which claim to be what they are not' cannot have full canonical status, those who doubt the Pauline authorship claimed by the Pastoral Epistles had better leave them 'out of their operative canon of Scripture until they come to a better mind and a surer faith'.[1] (Hebert puts 'saner' for 'surer', an unfortunate slip which imports a priggish note into Stibbs' remark.) Hebert's comment is this: 'Is he not assuming that all pseudonymous writings are "forgeries" in our sense of the word? and is he not applying a standard of apostolic authorship which would exclude from the canon at least the epistle to the Hebrews?' Hebert himself thinks (on 'critical grounds') that in the Pastorals 'it is not the real Paul . . . speaking to us, but someone else using his name'; but, he holds, 'this is not to say that they are "forgeries", that is to say, writings fraudulently drawn up to present a different teaching from St. Paul's.'

The first thing that must be said about this is that Hebert's Pickwickian definition of 'forgery' is entirely his own. The dictionary definition of 'forgery' is fraudulent imitation, as such, irrespective of its aim, the point of the fraud being simply to get one's own product accepted as somebody else's. Now, the Pastorals (unlike Hebrews, which makes no claim as to its authorship) tell us that they are by Paul, and hence by implication profess themselves to be invested with Paul's personal apostolic authority. On Hebert's view, they were not written by Paul, nor, presumably, with his sanction, or that of any apostle. They are, therefore, fraudulent; we must suppose (as Hebert seems to do) that the writer personated Paul in order that what he wrote might be regarded as having apostolic authority, to which he himself could not lay claim. Whether or not he incorporated genuine Pauline fragments, or reproduced the mind of Paul fairly, is neither here nor there; nor is it relevant to appeal to the fact (true though it is) that pseudonymous literary forms were common in the ancient world. The crucial point here is simply that by pretending to be Paul the writer sought to secure

[1] *Op. cit.*, p. 1063.

for his own work the unique and absolute authority which the early Church knew that Christ had given specifically to the apostles, and to them alone; and that he was no more entitled to do this than Hebert or I would be. On this view, the Pastorals are in truth a forgery and a fraud. And frauds are still fraudulent, even when perpetrated from noble motives, as Hebert thinks this one was.

When Stibbs judges that Epistles which originated in this way are not apostolic in such a sense that they could possibly be regarded as canonical, he is in line with historic catholic orthodoxy; the second-century Muratorian fragment specifies two alleged Epistles of Paul (to the Laodiceans and to the Alexandrians) which the early Church excluded from its canon because they were forged, and it is clear that, had the Pastorals been known to fall in the same category, they would have been rejected too. What is strange is not that Stibbs takes this line, but that Hebert should suppose that the authority of the Pastorals as canonical Scripture would not be affected if they were in fact pseudonymous. Such a view shows failure to understand two things : first, the unique personal authority and historical significance of the apostolate, and, second, the biblical concept of Scripture. For the first : if the Pastorals did not come from within the original apostolic circle, then they are no part of the authoritative exposition of the faith which Christ inspired His apostles to give for the guidance of the universal Church, and so they are not canonical. For the second : if the Pastorals are Scripture, then their claim to authorship, like all their other assertions, should be received as truth from God; and one who rejects this claim ought also to deny that they are Scripture, for what he is saying is that they have not the nature of Scripture, since they make false statements. Stibbs' position, that their canonicity cannot be affirmed if their authenticity is denied, thus seems to be the only one possible; and we may lay it down as a general principle that, when biblical books specify their own authorship, the affirmation of their canonicity involves a denial of their pseudonymity. Pseudonymity and canonicity are mutually exclusive.

In a footnote, Hebert dismisses 2 Peter with the comment: 'the same principles apply as in the case of the Pastorals.' This is true; and therefore if we are to regard 2 Peter as canonical we must regard it as apostolic also.

In view of the suspicion of Hebert and others that there is something arbitrary and dishonest about the evangelical attitude to the hypothesis of the pseudonymity of the books above mentioned, it may be helpful to conclude by showing what is the real state of the question with regard to it. As we have seen, if a New Testament book is not authentically apostolic, and if it makes false assertions (as on this hypothesis these books do), then it has not the nature of Scripture, and has no place in the New Testament canon. But the fact is that these books established their place in the canon of the early Church, and have been studied and expounded in the Church for centuries without anything unworthy of their apparent authors, or inconsistent with the rest of Scripture, either in teaching or in tone, being found in them. This fact alone is almost, if not quite, decisive; is it conceivable that this happened without the guidance and blessing of the Spirit, and indeed contrary to His leading?—for it is surely Satan, rather than the Spirit of God, who leads men to make false judgments as to what is Scripture and what is not! The presumption of authenticity is surely overwhelming. Some may still find themselves able to think it remotely possible that the Church has been misled here; but even if they do they can hardly think it likely. At all events, the *onus probandi* is on those who deny the traditional view. And it is not enough for them to produce evidence which *could* indicate pseudonymity; the evidence needs to be such as *must* indicate it, and cannot mean anything else, or else it will not be such as makes it reasonable to abandon a presumption which is so strong. As long as it is possible to explain the evidence adduced in a way compatible with authenticity, it will be right for us to do so. Any other course would be a breach of the rules of sound scholarship. It may safely be said that none of the evidence so far adduced is inexplicable, or even embarrassing, on the assumption of authenticity; and that it seems unlikely that stronger evidence will be forthcoming in the future. No adequate reason, therefore, exists for doubting the authenticity, and therefore the canonicity, of these books. The grounds on which many Christian scholars do in fact deny their authenticity appear insufficient to overthrow the enormous presumption in favour of it. The view of these scholars reflects failure to assess the strength of this presumption, a lapse due apparently to overlooking the fact that to deny authenticity is to deny canonicity also.

INDEX